T0290514

# The U.S. Experience with No-Fault Automobile Insurance

A Retrospective

James M. Anderson, Paul Heaton, Stephen J. Carroll

RAND INSTITUTE FOR CIVIL JUSTICE

The research described in this report was conducted within the RAND Institue for Civil Justice (ICJ). ICJ research is supported by pooled grants from corporations, trade and professional associations, and individuals; by government grants and contracts; and by private foundations.

Library of Congress Cataloging-in-Publication Data

Anderson, James M.
    The U.S. experience with no-fault automobile insurance : a
retrospective / James M. Anderson, Paul Heaton, Stephen J. Carroll.
    p. cm.
    Includes bibliographical references.
    ISBN 978-0-8330-4916-2 (pbk. : alk. paper)
    1. No-fault automobile insurance—Law and legislation—United States.
2. No-fault automobile insurance—United States. 3. Liability for traffic
accidents—United States. I. Heaton, Paul. II. Carroll, Stephen J., 1940– III. Title.

    KF1219.5.A96 2010
    346.73'0865728—dc22

                                                                2009047041

The RAND Corporation is a nonprofit research organization providing objective analysis and effective solutions that address the challenges facing the public and private sectors around the world. RAND's publications do not necessarily reflect the opinions of its research clients and sponsors. **RAND®** is a registered trademark.

*Cover image courtesy of Media Bakery.*

Published 2010 by the RAND Corporation
1776 Main Street, P.O. Box 2138, Santa Monica, CA 90407-2138
1200 South Hayes Street, Arlington, VA 22202-5050
4570 Fifth Avenue, Suite 600, Pittsburgh, PA 15213-2665
RAND URL: http://www.rand.org/
To order RAND documents or to obtain additional information, contact
Distribution Services: Telephone: (310) 451-7002;
Fax: (310) 451-6915; Email: order@rand.org

# Preface

Policymakers' choices about automobile-accident insurance are vitally important. These choices affect not only the world's largest insurance market but also incentives that may affect driving behavior—an activity that results in the deaths of more than 35,000 people every year in the United States. For policymakers to make those choices wisely, they need a thorough understanding of the advantages and disadvantages of the available policy options and a history of the debate. This monograph provides an overview of the United States' experience with its boldest experiment in the history of automobile insurance: no-fault automobile-insurance systems, in which automobile-accident victims seek compensation from their own insurer. It will be of interest not only to policymakers but also to researchers and insurers interested in no-fault insurance systems.

We build on a long history of RAND Institute for Civil Justice (ICJ) research to help policymakers more thoroughly understand the effect of policy choices in automobile insurance. From the rate of fraud to the effects of choice and no-fault insurance, ICJ has long provided independent analyses to aid policymakers in achieving an empirically grounded understanding of the issues. A full list of ICJ publications related to auto insurance is available from RAND Corporation (2009).

Questions or comments about this monograph should be sent to the project leader, James Anderson (James_Anderson@rand.org).

## The RAND Institute for Civil Justice

The mission of the RAND Institute for Civil Justice is to improve private and public decisionmaking on civil legal issues by supplying policymakers and the public with the results of objective, empirically based, analytic research. ICJ facilitates change in the civil justice system by analyzing trends and outcomes, identifying and evaluating policy options, and bringing together representatives of different interests to debate alternative solutions to policy problems. ICJ builds on a long tradition of RAND research characterized by an interdisciplinary, empirical approach to public policy issues and rigorous standards of quality, objectivity, and independence.

ICJ research is supported by pooled grants from corporations, trade and professional associations, and individuals; by government grants and contracts; and by private foundations. ICJ disseminates its work widely to the legal, business, and research communities and to the general public. In accordance with RAND Corporation policy, all ICJ research products are subject to peer review before publication. ICJ publications do not necessarily reflect the opinions or policies of the research sponsors or of the ICJ Board of Overseers.

Information about ICJ is available online (http://www.rand.org/icj/). Inquiries about research projects should be sent to the following address:

James Dertouzos, Director
RAND Institute for Civil Justice
1776 Main Street
P.O. Box 2138
Santa Monica, CA 90407-2138
310-393-0411 x7476
Fax: 310-451-6979
James_Dertouzos@rand.org

# Contents

# Figures

# Tables

# Summary

To many commentators and policymakers in the 1970s, it appeared as though no-fault automobile insurance was a genuinely superior policy innovation that would displace conventional tort-based automobile-insurance regimes. More than 30 years later, no-fault has lost much of its popularity among insurers and consumer groups. What happened? This monograph provides an overview of the experience in the United States with no-fault automobile insurance and the factors that led to its decline in popularity among insurers, consumer groups, and legislatures. We explore the history of no-fault and examine its performance relative to other approaches for automobile-accident compensation. We draw from a variety of data sources, including qualitative interviews, surveys, and administrative databases, to evaluate the successes and failures of no-fault and consider its likely future in the United States.

Prompted by dissatisfaction with the traditional tort system for compensating the ever-rising number of automobile-accident victims, no-fault proponents advocated a less adversarial approach. The central idea of a no-fault system is that, rather than seek recovery against another driver under conventional principles of tort law, an injured automobile-accident victim could simply recover the costs of the accident from his or her own insurance company.

This "no-fault" approach involves three components: (1) a partial or total restriction on the right to sue other drivers for being at fault for automobile accidents, (2) a restriction on recovering for pain and suffering or other noneconomic damages, and (3) mandatory insurance so that the victim can recover his or her economic losses (including medical costs) from his or her own insurance company. In the United States, *add-on no-fault* is an important variation in which an injured party can recover from his or her own automobile insurance without any restriction on also filing a tort claim against another driver. Another important variation, *choice*, allows individual drivers to choose whether to accept, in exchange for lower premiums, restrictions on their right to sue other drivers.

No-fault approaches to automobile insurance were first proposed in the 1920s, modeled after the workers' compensation no-fault approach to workplace accidents. For the next 40 years, numerous academic studies decried the use of the tort system to compensate injured victims of automobile accidents. Commentators focused on the following failings of the tort system:

(1) As a result of the fault standard, many victims were either not compensated at all or undercompensated. (2) There was a long delay in providing compensation to injured persons. (3) The seriously injured were often undercompensated while victims with minor injuries were often overcompensated. (4) The process of establishing fault created high administrative costs. (5) Victims and injurers had large incentives to be dishonest in their efforts to improve their cases. (R. Keeton and O'Connell, 1965, pp. 2–6)

Because it minimized litigation and administrative costs associated with determining who was at fault for an accident, supporters of no-fault supposed it to be less expensive than the tort system.

Massachusetts passed the nation's first no-fault automobile-insurance law in 1970, and many other states soon followed. A number of insurers and consumer groups supported no-fault over the opposition of the trial lawyers, and, for a while, it appeared as though it was a genuinely superior policy innovation.

Over time, however, dissatisfaction with no-fault grew, primarily because the hoped-for premium-cost reductions never materialized. Several states repealed no-fault laws and realized premium-cost reductions. Political debate about no-fault increasingly focused solely on the issue of consumer premium costs, and the other justifications for the no-fault approach on which its original proponents relied lost political salience. Many insurers and consumer groups that once supported no-fault as a means of reducing rate increases no longer support it.

We demonstrate that the perception that no-fault auto-insurance claim costs were higher than other auto-insurance systems was largely accurate. Total injury costs per insured vehicle gradually began to diverge across systems in the late 1980s, with no-fault becoming substantially more expensive than tort. Whereas injury costs under no-fault were only 12 percent higher in 1987 than those under tort, this difference had ballooned to 73 percent by 2004. Surprisingly, we also found that states that restricted lawsuits against other drivers—in an attempt to reduce costs—actually exhibited higher claim costs than states that permitted these lawsuits.

Why were no-fault regimes unexpectedly more expensive? We identify medical costs as a primary contributing factor. Medical treatment in no-fault states was vastly more expensive than in other states. Controlling for a broad range of personal and accident characteristics, we demonstrate that claimants in no-fault states are more likely to claim the use of virtually every type of medical provider, from emergency room to chiropractor, and visit each type of provider more frequently than claimants in other states. We also show that the same medical care costs more to the auto-insurance system in no-fault states than in tort states and that most of this cost divergence occurred during the 1990s. In particular, prior to 1987, medical charges to the auto-insurance system for individuals in no-fault states were only slightly higher (5.7 percent) than for comparably injured individuals in tort states. However, by 1997, the disparity had grown beyond 40 percent. While we discuss plausible explanations for these trends, further research is necessary to determine exactly why medical costs in no-fault states grew so dramatically during this period. One possibility is that no-fault insurance shifts medical costs associated with auto accidents from the first-party health-insurance system to the automobile-insurance system.

We also demonstrate that, while no-fault states had lower levels of litigation activity and devoted a smaller share of payments to non-economic damages in the 1980s than did tort states, by 2007, the two systems had largely converged on these characteristics. No-fault has shifted over time from a system with better medical benefits but reduced access to the courts to a system that simply offers more-generous medical benefits.

We conclude that the decline in no-fault's popularity is a result of (1) its unexpectedly high claim costs and (2) the political debate shifting from an overall assessment of the optimal insurance system to the impact of those high costs on consumers. No-fault's high claim costs are the result of very high medical costs. Further research is necessary to evaluate reforms that some no-fault states have introduced to control the growth of medical costs.

# Acknowledgments

We would like to thank all those who cooperated with our research team to make their insights and data available. The members of the ICJ Research Advisory Council were particularly helpful. David Corum at the Insurance Research Council provided valuable assistance in obtaining various data sets used in the monograph. We also appreciate the assistance of numerous interviewees from insurance companies and the legal and academic communities, many of whom were interviewed with the understanding that they would remain anonymous. We are grateful to James Dertouzos, Robert Reville, Fred Kipperman, and Eric Helland for their support and suggestions and to Michelle Platt for her administration of the project. We want to thank Susan Gates, the ICJ quality-assurance director, for her assistance in moving this project through the peer-review process. Finally, we are grateful to the reviewers, David Loughran and J. David Cummins, for their thoughtful comments and suggestions. We would also like to thank ICJ board member Robert Peck for his feedback. Thanks are also due to Laura Zakaras for her suggestions and to Lisa Bernard and Christina Pitcher for their skillful and meticulous editing.

# Abbreviations

| | |
|---|---|
| ABA | American Bar Association |
| ANF | absolute no-fault |
| BI | bodily injury |
| CDF | cumulative distribution function |
| EMS | emergency medical service |
| ER | emergency room |
| GPS | Global Positioning System |
| HMO | health maintenance organization |
| ICJ | RAND Institute for Civil Justice |
| IRC | Insurance Research Council |
| MCS | modification of the current system |
| MedPay | medical payment |
| NAACP | National Association for the Advancement of Colored People |
| NHTSA | National Highway Traffic Safety Administration |
| PD | property damage |
| PIP | personal-injury protection |

UIM          underinsured motorist

UM           uninsured motorist

# CHAPTER ONE

# Introduction

## Background

Tort-law scholar Guido Calabresi (1985, p. 1) once asked his readers to imagine an evil deity who demanded 55,000 lives every year in exchange for providing amazing powers of individual transportation without precedent in human history. The personal automobile is the evil deity to which he referred, and we have accepted the bargain but still struggle to allocate the overwhelming costs. In 2006 alone, a staggering 2,575,000 people were injured in automobile accidents in the United States, and 42,642 people were killed (NHTSA, 2008). This enormous toll has long represented the largest single source of accidental injury in the United States. The financial costs compound this human tragedy: Automobile crashes cost $241 billion in 2003, according to the National Safety Council.

The world's largest insurance market has developed as a result of this source of accidental injury and death. U.S. consumers spend more than $110 billion every year on liability insurance for auto accidents—a larger amount than for any other category of insurance expenditure (A. M. Best Company, 2008). Another result has been an enormous amount of litigation. Automobile-accident litigation makes up two-thirds of all injury claims, three-quarters of all lawyers' fees, and three-quarters of all payouts in the personal-injury liability system (Burke, 2002, p. 103). The result of the mixture of insurance and tort law has been a costly system that provides compensation that is very unevenly related to the injuries incurred by the victim.[1]

Commentators have been seeking a better way to allocate the costs of accidents and compensate victims since almost from the time that Henry Ford's Model T popularized the automobile—and the Mephistophelean bargain that went with it. Influenced by the example of workers' compensation laws that provided payment to injured workers without a showing of fault, commentators advocated a system of compensation that did not rely on the requirement that an injured party show the fault of another driver in order to gain compensation for his or her injuries (Carman, 1919; Marx, 1925; Committee to Study Compensation for Automobile Accidents, 1932). Beginning in 1919, they generally argued for an approach to compensation that did not rely on the tort system and reduced or eliminated compensation for noneconomic losses, such as pain and suffering, to accident victims with less serious injuries. In return, the system would provide assured compensation for accident victims' economic losses without regard for fault. Proponents of this approach argued that it would reduce the overall costs of the system and increase the fraction of the auto-insurance dollar that would go to injured people. The elimination of these disputes would also speed the provision of compensation. Compensation would, thus, be adequate to cover economic loss regardless of fault and would be more equitably distributed among injured parties. Around 1970, this system became known generally as a *no-fault system*.[2]

Between 1971 and 1976, 16 states adopted some form of mandatory no-fault compensation system. Nine other states either required the purchase of, or required that insurers offer, enhanced first-party insurance covering an insured's economic losses, without any constraint on access to the tort system. Early empirical evaluations of no-fault were generally positive, and it seemed likely that no-fault would be widely adopted.

---

[1]  Victims often receive compensation from other sources—most importantly, medical insurance.

[2]  Then–Massachusetts state legislator Michael Dukakis is credited with coining this name for the legislation he successfully pushed in the Massachusetts legislature.

Over time, however, insurer and consumer-group support waned—largely because the costs of no-fault remained higher than expected. Four states repealed their no-fault laws in the 1980s and 1990s. In California, political opponents of no-fault were able to defeat several well-funded efforts to enact a no-fault system. The Rhode Island legislature also considered no-fault at some length before rejecting it in 1993. In the wake of these defeats, some insurers reconsidered their earlier support for no-fault. Insurers were instrumental in the 2004 repeal of no-fault in Colorado and the near-repeal of no-fault in Florida. One commentator described "something of a backlash against no-fault" (Oliphant, 2007).

The rise and fall in support for no-fault raise some critical questions: Is no-fault a failed policy experiment? Or does it have a future, perhaps in some altered form? What conclusions can we draw from the American experience with no-fault automobile insurance?

While there is a substantial body of work on the costs of no-fault automobile insurance compared with those of tort, there has been little work done in the past five years on this issue. The field also lacks an overall retrospective of the experience in the United States with no-fault insurance that can provide a historical perspective on this policy question and help explain why no-fault was adopted, flourished, and then lost some of its political luster as a policy option.

## Research Purpose and Approach

This monograph is intended to provide a comprehensive look at the evolution of the no-fault system, a partial evaluation of its performance in comparison to the tort system, and a discussion of its potential future. Specifically, we address the following research questions:

- What are the key differences between the tort system and the no-fault approach to compensation, and what are the different forms of no-fault insurance in the United States?
- How did the no-fault system evolve, and why has it fallen from favor?

- How do the costs of no-fault approaches compare with the costs of the tort system in compensating injuries from automobile accidents?
- What are the causes of the rising costs associated with no-fault systems?
- What is the likely future of no-fault?

Our goal is not necessarily to provide a definitive assessment of the merits of the systems, but rather to understand the costs of no-fault and why no-fault has apparently lost support among politicians, insurers, and the public in the past 30 years.

To answer these questions, we used a number of research methods. Initially, we conducted a focus group with the RAND Institute of Civil Justice's Research Advisory Council, which consisted primarily of automobile-insurance stakeholders. This focus group helped us learn how the perceptions of no-fault automobile insurance had changed over time and generate plausible hypotheses about the claim costs of no-fault compared with those of tort. We reviewed the copious academic literature on no-fault automobile insurance to understand the goals of the early advocates for no-fault and to understand how the debate over no-fault insurance has shifted over time. We then conducted structured qualitative interviews with insurance-company representatives, consumer-group leaders, plaintiffs' lawyers, and academic experts in the field, many on a not-for-attribution basis. These interviews had two goals. First, we sought to identify plausible, testable empirical hypotheses to explain the patterns in insurance costs. Second, we sought to learn how perceptions of no-fault insurance have changed over time and understand the political history of no-fault.

Finally, we analyzed data from a variety of sources to examine how the functioning of the insurance regimes has changed over time. Our primary data sources included (1) closed (i.e., completed) claim data collected by the Insurance Research Council (IRC) between 1987 and 2007, with information on purchased policies, claimed injuries, and compensation amounts, and (2) consumer-panel surveys of individuals involved in automobile accidents, conducted on behalf of IRC in 1986, 1992, 1998, and 2002. We also examined data from the Civil

Justice Survey of State Courts, the National Center for State Courts' State Court Processing Statistics series, and the Fast Track Monitoring System. These rich sets of data allowed us to analyze and trace the changes in the operation of automobile-insurance regimes over the past 20 years and compare no-fault with other regimes.

We offer two caveats about the scope of our research. First, we limit our research to the United States. Many countries have adopted no-fault automobile-insurance systems, and we make no effort in this monograph to examine these systems. Second, while we find that no-fault automobile-insurance costs rose as a result of medical costs incurred from automobile crashes, further research is necessary to analyze the relationship between automobile insurance and medical insurance and the means by which the systems affect one another. In particular, in this monograph, we do not evaluate the extent to which no-fault shifts costs between auto insurers, medical insurers, medical providers, and the government. Instead, we limit our focus to costs borne within the auto-insurance system—the costs that have been most salient in political debates surrounding auto-insurance reform.

## Organization of This Monograph

Chapter Two explains the basic kinds of automobile insurance, addresses the differences between the tort system and the no-fault system, and describes how many variations of the no-fault approach exist in the United States. This chapter is important background for the empirical analysis, which compares the cost increases not just between tort and no-fault systems but among different types of no-fault approaches. The intellectual and political history of no-fault is outlined in Chapter Three, from the development of no-fault in the workers' compensation context to its recent decline in popularity. Chapter Four explains how the data show that policy costs under no-fault have increased more than under tort. Chapter Five analyzes possible explanations for these cost trends and concludes that many are attributable to rising medical costs. Finally, Chapter Six offers a short summary, discusses some promising policy approaches, explores the implications for no-fault of some likely developments in auto insurance, and identifies other areas for further research.

CHAPTER TWO
# A Primer on Tort and No-Fault Systems

To understand the rise and partial decline of the popularity of no-fault and understand the changing patterns of costs discussed in Chapters Four and Five, one must first understand the different kinds of automobile-insurance regimes used by different states. These can be roughly divided into tort and no-fault. Under a conventional tort regime, a victim recovers compensation from another party (or, almost invariably, the other party's insurer) if the victim can show that the other party was at fault for the accident. Under a tort system, a consumer purchases automobile insurance primarily to protect himself or herself from having to pay for the harms caused by his or her at-fault accidents. In contrast, under a no-fault regime, a victim of an automobile accident usually recovers costs primarily from his or her own automobile insurer. In a pure no-fault system, it is neither necessary nor even possible to sue other parties for the costs associated with automobile accidents. The consumer purchases automobile insurance to insure himself or herself against his or her costs from accidents. The two systems and their many variations are described in more detail in this chapter. We reserve a discussion of historical arguments for and against these regimes for Chapter Three.

## Conventional Tort Approaches to Automobile Insurance

Under traditional tort common-law principles, individuals and corporations are civilly liable for certain harms ("torts") that they cause. The wrongdoer must compensate the victim for the costs suffered. How-

7

ever, not every harm is a tort. The traditional elements of a negligent tort are the existence of a duty, the breach of that duty, causation, and injury. Thus, to avoid being found negligent, a driver must not breach his or her duty to take reasonable care in the operation of the automobile. If the driver does so, he or she is liable for injuries that he or she proximately causes in violation of this duty of reasonable care.

In practice, widespread insurance use has influenced the actual operation of the traditional system of liability in several important ways.[1] First, insurance adjusters have adopted rules (e.g., drivers who rear-end other vehicles are at fault) to allocate fault. These have minimized more-general analyses of reasonableness and causation in most automobile-accident cases, which are resolved without formal litigation. Rather than undertake a generalized analysis of whether a driver is negligent and therefore liable for an accident—a potentially difficult and open-ended inquiry—an insurance adjuster is likely to refer to a simpler set of rules to determine who owes what to whom (Hensler et al., 1991; Ross, 1980, p. 237 ["The law of negligence was made to lean heavily upon the much simpler traffic law"]).[2] Second, the fact that drivers in most states are required to carry insurance has resulted in the vast majority of litigation being focused on other drivers rather than other parties (e.g., auto manufacturers, municipalities) whose decisions may have contributed to auto accidents. The existence of widespread automobile insurance also contributed to the development of lawyers who specialize in such cases (Abraham, 2008). Finally, the amount of

---

[1]   Today, every state except Florida, New Hampshire, and Wisconsin requires automobile liability insurance (Insurance Information Institute, 2009). In Florida, New Hampshire, and Wisconsin, purchasing insurance is the easiest way to meet the state's financial-responsibility law. Each of these states has financial-responsibility laws that can be satisfied by auto insurance, a surety bond, personal funds, or a certificate of self-insurance (Fla. Stat. §324.031; Wis. Stat. §344.14; N.H. Stat. §264:20).

Until the 1970s, most states simply had laws that required financial responsibility rather than mandatory insurance. Massachusetts passed the first mandatory-insurance law in 1925. For more than 30 years, it was the only state with mandatory insurance until New York passed a similar bill in 1956 (Abraham, 2008, pp. 72–74).

[2]   See also Schwartz (2000, p. 614), who argued that the "almost comprehensive" motor-vehicle code had the effect that auto tort cases cost less to resolve than other kinds of tort cases.

insurance that the defendant possesses usually serves as a de facto cap on damages. Under the law, an automobile operator is personally liable for whatever losses that he or she causes, whether or not he or she has adequate insurance. However, research has shown that recoveries over insurance policy limits—called "blood money"—are rarely sought by plaintiffs or their attorneys (T. Baker, 2001, p. 281).

When fault is shared by more than one party, different states have adopted different compensation rules. Historically, a plaintiff who was even slightly at fault could not recover anything, under the rule of contributory negligence. The defendant could raise contributory negligence as a defense, and, if the defendant could show that the plaintiff was even slightly negligent, recovery would be completely denied. Today, almost every state has adopted some form of comparative negligence to ameliorate the harshness of the rule of contributory negligence. Under comparative negligence, a judgment against a liable defendant can be reduced proportionally to the degree to which the plaintiff was at fault.[3]

Under the traditional tort system, several insurance options for covering the risk of automobile tort liability have developed.[4] These include the following:

---

[3] Under pure comparative negligence, the plaintiff can recover whatever percentage of the fault for which he or she was not responsible. So, if the plaintiff was 90 percent responsible for the accident, he or she could still recover 10 percent from the defendant. Many other states adopted a more limited form of comparative negligence, which allows recovery by the plaintiff only if his or her negligence was not greater than the defendant's. Under these rules, if a plaintiff was either at least 50 percent or 51 percent (depending on the particular state's law) responsible for the injury, he or she could not recover. This is a compromise between the traditional contributory-negligence rule and pure comparative negligence.

Interestingly, the adoption of comparative negligence by statute was partially driven by opponents of no-fault automobile insurance. No-fault proponents used the harshness of the traditional rule to argue for the adoption of no-fault. By ameliorating the perceived unfairness of the traditional rule, no-fault proponents hoped to remove an argument for no-fault (Franklin, Rabin, and Green, 2006, p. 446).

[4] We exclude discussion of property damages from automobile accidents because property damages are treated more uniformly across liability systems and make up a relatively small fraction of overall costs.

- *Bodily injury* (BI) insurance pays the liabilities incurred by the automobile operator who has the insurance (i.e., the insured) for any damages that he or she owes for injuring another person. BI can include economic damages (e.g., medical bills and lost income) and noneconomic damages, also known as *general damages* (e.g., pain and suffering and loss of consortium). In practice, the injured party or that party's attorney files a claim directly with the driver's insurance company. This is *third-party insurance*, which is in contrast to *first-party insurance*, in which the insured's own insurance pays benefits directly to him. The coverage is usually sold with different available upper limits. Some form of BI insurance is mandatory in most states. BI insurance is most important and is the primary coverage in tort states—states that have not adopted no-fault coverage.[5]

- *Medical-payment* (MedPay) coverage compensates the insured for any medical costs that he or she incurs.[6] It is generally optional and usually has relatively low policy limits (often $5,000 or $10,000). Because it is paid to the insured party (rather than to the victim injured by the insured), it is called *first-party insurance*. In tort states, it is sometimes thought to act as a speedy adjunct to immediately pay medical bills while the larger claim against the at-fault driver is litigated or settled, a process that can be comparatively slow.

- *Uninsured-motorist/underinsured-motorist* (UM/UIM) coverage compensates the insured for losses that result if the insured is injured by another driver who is uninsured or underinsured. The insured can recover from his or her own insurance company the losses that he or she would have been able to recover against the at-fault driver had that driver been adequately insured. It is first-party coverage (because the driver recovers from his or

---

[5]  BI coverage is also required in no-fault states to cover accidents that might exceed the tort threshold.

[6]  MedPay coverage was first offered in 1941, initially available only to help the nonfamily passengers in the insured driver's auto. In 1953, it was made available to cover the driver and his or her family (Abraham, 2008, p. 79). The initial limitation to nonfamily members was to reduce the risk of moral hazard and possible collusive accidents.

her own insurance), but it mimics ordinary tort liability in its coverage. The underinsured at-fault party is still legally liable to the insured for whatever injuries he or she caused. As a practical matter, however, if the driver is uninsured, he is also likely to be "judgment proof" (i.e., poor and not worth suing). In the unlikely event that the insured recovers in tort against the underinsured motorist, the insurer would be entitled to recoup from this recovery any funds that it paid out.[7]

## No-Fault Approaches to Automobile Insurance

The no-fault approach to compensation emphasizes providing compensation more broadly than in the tort approach, without restricting it to those who can prove that another party was negligent or at fault for the accident.[8] Compensation is usually restricted to economic loss. Noneconomic loss, such as pain and suffering or loss of consortium, is excluded or limited, as explained in this section.

Some proponents of no-fault systems envisioned completely abolishing conventional third-party liability of another driver, akin to workers' compensation abolishment of employer liability. If one was injured in an auto accident, one would recover from one's own insurance company, and there would be no need to sue anyone. While that approach has been adopted in New Zealand, Saskatchewan, Quebec,

---

[7] Interestingly, UIM coverage developed after the insurance industry successfully opposed an effort in New York State to require liability coverage. The superintendent of insurance asked the industry to propose a solution (other than mandatory insurance) to the problem of uninsured drivers (Widiss, 1985, pp. 10–11).

In regions with large numbers of uninsured motorists or states in which the mandatory minimums are low, UM/UIM insurance can be critical. One plaintiff's lawyer we interviewed emphasized the importance of this coverage in litigation.

[8] While no-fault and first-party payer systems have been historically linked, it would be possible to have a no-fault third-party system (e.g., workers' compensation) or a first-party system in which the victim had to prove that someone else was at fault (which is how UM/UIM insurance operates).

Israel, and some European jurisdictions, it has not been tried in the United States.[9]

Instead, in the United States, no-fault regimes are accompanied by limitations on the right to sue for bodily injuries rather than total abolition of third-party liability. The limitations prevent suit unless the injury exceeds either a *monetary threshold* or a *verbal threshold*:

- *Monetary thresholds* are tied to the amount of damages suffered by the victim and require the victim to exceed a particular threshold in order to sue in tort against the tortfeasor. For example, in Massachusetts, a state with a monetary threshold, a victim's injuries must total $2,000 in order for him or her to sue in the tort system. In most states, thresholds are fixed by statute. Because of inflation of medical costs, over time, a higher proportion of cases will exceed the fixed threshold unless the legislature adjusts the threshold.

- *Verbal thresholds* require a particular level of seriousness of the injury, which is defined by statute and case law. For example, in New York, injuries must be "serious" in order for a victim to sue in tort.[10]

---

[9] See Schuck (2008) for a discussion of the New Zealand system and Kretzmer (1976) for a discussion of the Israeli system. Outreville (1984) explains the effect of no-fault in Quebec.

[10] New York statute defines *serious injury* as

> a personal injury which results in death; dismemberment; significant disfigurement; a fracture; loss of a fetus; permanent loss of use of a body organ, member, function or system; permanent consequential limitation of use of a body organ or member; significant limitation of use of a body function or system; or a medically determined injury or impairment of a non-permanent nature which prevents the injured person from performing substantially all of the material acts which constitute such person's usual and customary daily activities for not less than ninety days during the one hundred eighty days immediately following the occurrence of the injury or impairment. (N.Y. Stat. §5102[d])

Other examples of the language found in the various verbal thresholds in use as of this writing are as follows: "death" (all), "significant and permanent loss of an important bodily function" (Florida, Fla. Stat. §627.737), "permanent serious disfigurement" (Michigan, Mich. Comp. Laws §500.3135; Pennsylvania, 75 Pa. C.S. §1602), and "dismemberment" (New Jersey, 39 N.J.S. 6A-8).

In general, verbal thresholds are thought to be more effective in keeping cases out of the tort system because they are more rigid. With a monetary threshold, a victim can exceed the threshold by incurring additional costs (e.g., receiving more medical care). The rigidity of a verbal threshold depends, however, on how the relevant state supreme court interprets the verbal threshold. In Pennsylvania, for example, a "serious bodily injury" exceeds the threshold. The definition of *serious bodily injury* is up to the particular fact finder and depends on the injury's specific effect on the particular victim.[11] As one plaintiffs' lawyer explained, "the cases are all over the map—a herniated disk can be a serious injury—it depends on how it affects the individual" (Madden, 2008). Thus, the extent to which a verbal threshold precludes tort suits depends on how the courts interpret the language of the threshold.[12]

Why do thresholds matter so much? Injured victims whose cases exceed the threshold and can show fault can recover noneconomic damages (e.g., pain and suffering). These noneconomic damages are sometimes substantially more than the economic damages.

*Personal-injury protection (PIP)* is the chief no-fault insurance product. It pays the insured for his or her economic losses, including

---

[11] According to *Washington v. Baxter*, 553 Pa. 434 (1998), the definition of *serious injury* depends on (1) the particular body function impaired, (2) the extent of the impairment, (3) the length of time the impairment lasted, (4) the treatment required to correct the impairment, and (5) any other relevant factor.

[12] In Pennsylvania, if a victim has elected limited tort, some attorneys will actually wait to see whether the victim eventually develops serious bodily injuries before taking the case. This, in turn, can provide incentives for the victim to engage in unnecessary medical care to strengthen a claim of serious bodily injuries and access to the tort system.

Counterintuitively, the more *first*-party insurance the victim has, the greater the likelihood that the victim will sue in tort. The more first-party insurance, the more medical care it is possible for the victim to use. The more ongoing medical care the victim can cite, the more likely the fact finder will determine that it is a serious medical injury and thus permit access to tort. One plaintiffs' lawyer we interviewed described a client whose efforts to show that her injuries crossed the tort threshold were hampered by the fact that she had stopped treating the injuries after her first-party medical benefit policy limit was reached.

Another hypothesis offered to explain the relationship between first-party medical insurance and tort claims is that, without first-party medical insurance, victims may need to accept a poor settlement offer from the third-party insurer in order to immediately pay medical bills.

lost income and cost of medical services, regardless of fault. Importantly, it does *not* cover noneconomic damages, defined as compensation for nonmonetary losses, such as pain, suffering, emotional distress, loss of society and companionship, loss of consortium, and loss of enjoyment of life. Since it pays the owner of the insurance policy for injuries suffered by the owner, it is first-party insurance. This is in contrast to third-party insurance, which is required in conventional tort states and which pays victims whom the insured has injured. It is often sold with varying dollar limits but is mandatory in no-fault states, since it is designed to substitute for recovery through the tort system.[13]

## Variations on No-Fault and Tort Approaches

While automobile-insurance regimes are often divided into tort and no-fault, there are a number of possible variations. A conventional no-fault system has three components: (1) a limitation on the ability to sue under the tort system, (2) a limitation on recovery for noneconomic damages, and (3) a first-party insurance system designed to replace the right to sue. While often spoken of together as being part of a no-fault system, these three components are independent of one another.

### Add-On Coverage

Other states are known as *add-on states* because the first-party no-fault coverage is added on to the conventional tort liability system and its required insurance coverages.

- *Mandatory add-on* requires drivers to purchase this first-party coverage in addition to conventional third-party liability coverage.
- *Optional add-on* requires insurance companies to offer first-party policies to drivers, who can choose or decline to purchase the coverage.

---

[13] PIP is similar to MedPay in that they are both first-party coverages that do not require any proof of fault. They differ in that PIP typically has much higher policy limits and provides more-comprehensive benefits (including, for example, rehabilitative services and lost income) than MedPay.

In these states, there is no restriction on access to the tort system or noneconomic damages through the tort system.

In conventional tort states, first-party PIP coverage is often available as an optional product, depending on the insurer. The insurer is not required to offer it, but insurers often do. This narrows the distinction between optional–add-on states and tort states.

### Choice

A few states—Kentucky,[14] New Jersey, and Pennsylvania—have a choice system that allows drivers to choose between less-expensive *limited tort insurance* (which restricts the right to recover for noneconomic losses) and more-expensive *full tort insurance* (which allows the insured to retain the full right to recover in tort against third parties).[15] When a driver who has elected full tort is injured by a driver who has elected limited tort, the full tort driver can recover against the limited-tort driver's BI insurance.[16] The limited-tort driver can recover against the other driver only for economic damages that exceed the limited-tort driver's PIP insurance coverage.

---

[14] Although Kentucky is technically a choice state, because motorists must specially file a form with the Office of Insurance in order to opt-out of the no-fault system, more than 90 percent of motorists are covered under no-fault. Thus, in practical terms, Kentucky functions like a no-fault state.

[15] Washington, D.C., also has elements of a choice system, but it is unique in that accident victims are permitted to choose, on an accident-by-accident basis, between PIP benefits and tort recovery.

[16] Interestingly, the benefits of the reduced liability associated with the limited tort option do not necessarily accrue to the limited-tort driver's insurer, which is still fully liable to the full-tort driver. This problem with existing choice plans has been criticized by Kinzler (2006, p. 37).

The federal choice plan, which is discussed in Chapter Three, addresses this problem by requiring full-tort drivers to purchase first-party *tort maintenance insurance*, which operates similarly to UM coverage. Under that proposed system, a driver who elects tort and who is in an accident with a driver who elects no-fault would recover against his or her own insurer under this coverage.

## A Typology of Auto-Insurance Regimes

Table 2.1 shows some of the possible automobile-insurance system variations.

In theory, there could also be limited-tort suits or noneconomic damages in automobile-accident cases without requiring any first-party insurance; however, no state has adopted such an approach.[17] Conversely, a state could require first-party insurance to cover noneconomic damages while still limiting or eliminating tort recovery against third parties. In addition, a number of untried policy options exist

**Table 2.1**
**Automobile-Insurance System Variations**

| System | Required First-Party Insurance | No Required First-Party Insurance |
|---|---|---|
| No tort; no noneconomic damages | True no-fault | Unused |
| Threshold based; limitation on tort and noneconomic damages | Conventional no-fault[a] | Unused |
| Optional limitation on tort and noneconomic damages | Choice | Unused |
| No limitation on tort or noneconomic damages | Mandatory add-on[b] | Conventional tort[c] Optional add-on[d] |

[a] The following states have no-fault systems that place some limitation on the right to sue in the tort system and require some form of first-party insurance: Florida, Hawaii, Kansas, Massachusetts, Michigan, Minnesota, New York, North Dakota, and Utah. Hawaii, Kansas, Kentucky, Massachusetts, Minnesota, North Dakota, and Utah have monetary thresholds. Florida, Michigan, and New York have verbal severity thresholds.

[b] Oregon, Delaware, and New Hampshire require the purchase of add-on policies.

[c] States with traditional tort auto-insurance regimes include Alabama, Alaska, Arizona, California, Colorado, Connecticut, Georgia, Idaho, Illinois, Indiana, Iowa, Louisiana, Maine, Mississippi, Missouri, Montana, Nebraska, Nevada, New Mexico, North Carolina, Ohio, Oklahoma, Rhode Island, Tennessee, Vermont, West Virginia, and Wyoming.

[d] These states include Arkansas, Maryland, South Carolina, South Dakota, Texas, Virginia, Washington, and Wisconsin.

---

[17] Some states generally limit noneconomic damages in all personal-injury suits to a statutorily fixed sum.

that mix different combinations of the limitation on tort, limitation on noneconomic damages, and first-party insurance, the three constitutive elements of the no-fault approach.

## Conclusion

This chapter reviewed the types of automobile-insurance regimes used in the United States and the primary insurance products that are used in each type of regime.

While this typology of regimes accurately describes the relevant legal requirements in each state, the details of each regime vary widely by state and can cause states ostensibly under one system to closely resemble those under a different regime. For example, in some states with low monetary thresholds, the threshold is exceeded in most accidents. Since the victim can sue in tort in addition to recovering against his or her first-party insurer when the threshold is exceeded, a low–monetary threshold state can resemble a mandatory–add-on state in practice.

Other state-by-state details also vary widely. There are substantial differences in required policy minimums between no-fault and tort states. Similarly, the range of median insurance coverage purchased by insureds who are involved in a claim varies from $40,000 in Massachusetts to $300,000 in a number of other states. The appendix contains a table detailing the specific insurance requirements in each state and the median coverage actually purchased.

# CHAPTER THREE

# A Brief History of No-Fault

To understand the history of no-fault automobile insurance and political arguments over its desirability, one must understand the emergence of the fault-based system of tort law itself. This chapter briefly sketches the intellectual and political history of no-fault automobile insurance, beginning with the emergence of fault-based liability.

Following the growth in automobile accidents, reformers proposed an alternative to the tort system that would promise quicker, fairer, less-expensive compensation to victims of the increasingly frequent automobile accident. After decades of rising accidents and tort costs, the first no-fault law went into effect in the United States in 1971 in Massachusetts (Mass. Gen. Laws ch. 90 §§34A–34R). In the 1970s, many other states followed, and no-fault proposals were widely debated. Early empirical evaluations of no-fault were generally positive. Over time, however, insurer and consumer-group support waned because the costs of no-fault remained higher than expected. Today, the auto-insurance regime seems stable in most states. While there is little political enthusiasm to enact no-fault in other states, there is little pressure to repeal it in most no-fault states.

## The Emergence of Fault and No-Fault: 1875–1915

To understand the contemporary debate over fault and no-fault automobile-insurance regimes, it is helpful to understand how the concept of fault and no-fault emerged. Given fault's current central status in U.S. tort law, it is easy to imagine that a plaintiff has always needed to prove fault as a prerequisite to liability and that liability without fault was a recent invention. However, many commentators believe that the requirement that a plaintiff must prove the defendant's fault as a prerequisite to liability emerged in the late 19th century (Schwartz, 1981, p. 1722).

Until recently, the conventional historical wisdom was that, prior to the 19th century, proving fault was not necessary in order to recover in the antecedents to modern tort (Schwartz, 1981, p. 1722; Gregory, 1951, pp. 361–362; Malone, 1970). In this limited sense, *all* tort law was no-fault. In the Whig version of this history of tort law, the development of the principle that a plaintiff must show fault in order to recover is a sign of Anglo-American law's moral development.[1] One turn-of-the-century commentator explained the superiority of the principle of fault as follows: "As early law is formal and unmoral, so the child or youth is wont to be technical at the expense of fairness" (Ames, 1908, p. 101).[2] In this view, the emergence of the requirement that a plaintiff must prove that the defendant was at fault in the United States in the second half of the 19th century was a sign of the moral

---

[1]   More recently, scholars have challenged this history of English common law (and the underlying teleological understanding of the law's moral development) on a number of grounds. Some have accepted the historical claim but rejected the teleology and suggested that the early English common law cleverly anticipated the later positive development of no-fault systems. Others have argued that some analogue to the idea of fault was, in fact, operative in the early cases (Schwartz, 1981, p. 1722; J. Baker, 1990, p. 456). See also Gilles (1994), who argued that English precedents expressed neither conventional negligence nor strict liability but fell between, focusing on an avoidability criterion. Still others have suggested that the preindustrial era was committed to a no-liability approach as a subsidy to emerging companies (Rabin, 1981).

[2]   See also Ames (1908, p. 113): "It is obvious that the spirit of reform which during the last six hundred years has been bringing our system of law more and more into harmony with moral principles has not yet achieved its perfect work."

progress of the U.S. legal system.[3] Remnants of this hostility to liability without fault can be seen in arguments against no-fault to this day.[4]

While the fault principle, therefore, seemed established at the turn of the century, a challenge to this principle soon arose. Increasing industrialization led to an ever-increasing number of serious injuries. Progressive Era social reformers successfully pressed for the removal of some defenses against negligence suits brought to court by injured workers.[5] Faced with increasing uncertainty and increased liability expenses, some employers joined workers and social reformers in supporting the passage of a no-fault workers' compensation system, modeled after a version enacted in England in 1897.[6] Between 1910 and 1921, all but five states adopted workers' compensation laws (Fishback and Kantor, 2000, p. 3).

The idea of liability without fault that underlay workmen's compensation laws was controversial. The highest court in New York State was so wedded to the importance of fault that it initially held the New York workers' compensation statute unconstitutional:

> If the argument in support of this statute is sound we do not see why it cannot logically be carried much further. Poverty and mis-

---

[3] The conventional citation is to Massachusetts Chief Justice Lemuel Shaw's opinion in *Brown v. Kendall*, (60 Mass. 292, 1850), as the leading early case that affirmed the principle that no negligence would lie without fault (Epstein, 1980, p. 772; Holmes, 1881, p. 105).

[4] The idea that fault is central to tort is associated with the idea that the chief function of tort law is corrective justice. Proponents of the deterrence or compensation functions of tort law (like some no-fault proponents) are less likely to be enamored of fault as a prerequisite to recovery (e.g., Calabresi, 1970).

[5] There were three defenses that made recovery difficult. The *fellow-servant rule* made it impossible to recover if the victim's injury was caused by the negligence of another worker instead of the employer. *Voluntary assumption of the risk* precluded recovery if the worker voluntarily assumed the risk in some way. Finally, *contributory negligence* barred recovery if the injured worker was in any way negligent, even if his or her negligence was far less than that of the employer.

[6] Statute of 1897, 60 and 61 Vict., ch. 37; Statute of 1906, 6 Edward VII, ch. 58. The English version was, in turn, influenced by the passage of the Employers' Liability Law of 1871 and Accident Insurance Bill of 1884 in Germany (Haller, 1988). Even earlier than 1897, English pirates agreed on a proto–workers' compensation system to compensate crew members if they became injured or disabled (Talty, 2007).

fortune from every cause are detrimental to the state . . . . If the legislature can say to an employer, "you must compensate your employee for an injury not caused by you or by your fault," why can it not go further and say to the man of wealth, "you have more property than you need and your neighbor is so poor that he can barely subsist; in the interest of natural justice you must divide with your neighbor so that he and his dependents shall not become a charge upon the State?". . . In its final and simple analysis that is taking the property of A and giving it to B, and that cannot be done under our Constitutions. (*Ives v. South B. R. Co.*, 94 N.E. 431 (1911, p. 440)

In New York, it was necessary to amend the state constitution to over-come this objection (Art. I, §1919).[7]

Prominent members of the legal academe were also skeptical of liability without fault. Harvard Law School professor Jeremiah Smith stated (1914, pp. 238–239),

[T]he rule of liability adopted by the statute (liability for damage irrespective of fault) is in direct conflict with the fundamental rule of the modern common law as to ordinary requisites of tort. In truth, the statute rejects the test prevailing in the courts in A.D. 1900 and comes much nearer to endorsing the test which used to prevail in A.D. 1400 [i.e., liability without fault].

To Smith, requiring fault as a prerequisite to liability was a sign of moral progress over the barbarism of liability without fault, and an abandonment of fault marked a return to this benighted era.

Smith further argued that the passage of the workers' compensa-tion bills posed a fundamental challenge to the principle of fault and warned that the two systems could not easily coexist. Anticipating no-fault insurance, he warned that there would soon be movement toward a more general social insurance scheme for all kinds of injuries, includ-ing those outside the workplace (J. Smith, 1914).

---

[7] The new workers' compensation statutes survived federal constitutional scrutiny (*New York Central Railroad v. White*, 243 U.S. 188, 1916).

## As Automobile Accidents Increased, Academics Recommended Extending a No-Fault Workers' Compensation Approach to Compensating Victims of Automobile Accidents: 1915–1940

Smith's warning that there would soon be broader proposals for no-fault insurance was prophetic. Numerous academics proposed no-fault approaches in settings other than the workplace.[8] Automobile accidents seemed like a particularly promising context in which to use a no-fault approach, and there were several proposals (e.g., Carman, 1919; Rollins, 1919; French, 1933).

Why apply the no-fault approach to automobile accidents? Like industrial accidents, they represented a new and growing source of injury. The profusion of the private automobile vastly increased the damage and injuries that an individual was able and likely to cause. The growth in the automobile sector was rapid. In 1900, there were just 8,000 automobiles registered in the United States. By 1915, there were 2 million; by 1920, 9 million, and, by 1930, 23 million automobiles on U.S. roads (DOT, 2003). Because of its weight and speed, an automobile was able to inflict much more damage than a horse-drawn carriage. Intersection controls and safety engineering were primitive or nonexistent. As a result, more than 30,000 people were killed in auto accidents in 1930. This was a fatality rate more than 20 times higher than today's (Abraham, 2008, pp. 70–71).[9] The automobile fatality rate increased more than five times from 1913 to 1932, while the death rate from other accidents showed a decline of 20 percent (Y. Smith, Lilly, and Dowling, 1932, p. 786).

There were few sources from which the injured or survivors could recover. Private health insurance was rare; social security nonexistent. Few drivers carried insurance, and many were effectively judgment proof. Even if an accident could be attributed to the negligent con-

---

[8]   For example, Ballantine (1916), who covered railway accidents.

[9]   In 1930, there were 28 deaths for 100 million miles driven. In 2008, there were 1.46 deaths per 100 million miles driven (Abraham, 2008, p. 71).

struction of an automobile, a victim was unable to recover against the auto manufacturer.[10]

The first automobile liability insurance policy was provided to Truman J. Martin by the Travelers Insurance Company in 1898 (Nordman, 1998, p. 459). Originally, liability coverage was provided under a "teams" policy, which was designed for horse-drawn vehicles. By 1905, a distinct policy for autos became widely available, and, by 1921, premiums for auto insurance amounted to $64 million. By 1930, premiums for auto insurance reached $177.5 million in 1921 dollars (Abraham, 2008, p. 71).

Despite this growth in liability insurance, many victims of automobile accidents remained wholly uncompensated (Committee to Study Compensation for Automobile Accidents, 1932, pp. 55–56). There was no requirement that auto operators carry liability insurance, and many did not. First-party health insurance was also very uncommon. In some states, beginning with Connecticut, in 1925, financial-responsibility laws were passed.[11] These required drivers who were in accidents to post a bond or procure liability insurance in order to retain the right to drive. These laws did nothing, however, to help victims injured in a driver's first accident, since the financial-responsibility laws applied only after a first accident:

> It was, after all, thin comfort for [the victim] to know that the drunken driver who had maimed him would have to insure for the protection of future victims or have his driver's license revoked. (R. Keeton and O'Connell, 1965, p. 104)

---

[10] Prior to Benjamin Cardozo's landmark opinion in *MacPherson v. Buick Motor Co.*, 111 N.E. 1050 (Ct. App. N.Y., 1916), victims injured by the negligence of the auto manufacturer were unable to recover against the manufacturer because the victim was not in privity of contract with the manufacturer. That is, because the manufacturer did not sell the product directly to the victim (but rather to the dealer), the manufacturer owed no duty of care to the ultimate consumer. The *MacPherson* approach—eliminating privity of contract as a prerequisite to sue—was ultimately adopted by every state.

[11] By 1932, 18 states had adopted financial-responsibility laws (Abraham, 2008, p. 73).

Nor did the laws do anything to help victims involved in single-car accidents or those who were unable to prove negligence against a third party.

Surprisingly, auto insurers actively *opposed* laws requiring that drivers purchase automobile liability insurance as a condition of driving (see, e.g., Sherman, 1929). J. Dewey Dorsett, general manager of the Association of Casualty and Surety Companies wrote, in his annual report,

> I doubt there is a person in this room who does not recognize, as I do, that recent efforts to promote compulsory automobile insurance laws, involving the introduction of bills in an unprecedented number of legislatures and the widespread use of publicity, confront the casualty side of our business with one of its more serious threats in two decades . . . . It began in Ohio and . . . it took all the ingenuity we could command to stop it there. Then it showed up in New York, and more recently has jumped to New Jersey, Connecticut, Vermont and Michigan. (Dorsett, 1950, pp. 6–7)

Insurers reasoned that such a mandate would be accompanied by regulation and that they might be prohibited from charging high-risk drivers a sufficiently high premium.[12] By 1927, only Massachusetts had adopted compulsory liability insurance (Abraham, 2008, p. 73). The experience in Massachusetts confirmed auto insurers' fears, with the insurers' payouts being substantially higher than expected during the years immediately following the introduction of mandatory insurance.

While there had been earlier suggestions to apply a workers' compensation no-fault approach to automobile accidents, the most influential was that of the Committee to Study Compensation for Automobile Accidents. The committee's 1932 report widely criticized the existing

[12] Even as recently as 2004, insurance trade groups have opposed mandatory automobile insurance. "[While] unlicensed and uninsured drivers are involved in more than 20 percent of the fatal crashes on America's highways, . . . compulsory auto insurance laws do not prevent uninsured drivers from owning or operating a vehicle" ("Mandatory Auto Insurance," 2004, quoting Laura Kotelman, senior counsel, Property Casualty Insurers Association of America).

system of compensation for automobile accidents.[13] The authors found that payments were disproportionately and irrationally distributed:

> [T]emporary disability cases with small losses are considerably overpaid, those with larger losses are slightly overpaid, while permanent disability cases of earners—the class with the largest losses and greatest need—receive just about enough to meet the losses incurred up to the time of our investigations and get nothing to apply against the continued medical expense or wage loss resulting from their impaired earning ability.

This finding of disproportionality between accident loss and payments would later be replicated by other studies of tort-based automobile-insurance compensation system.

The committee's study also emphasized the role that liability insurance plays in compensating auto-accident victims. If the other driver in an auto accident had liability insurance, some payment was received in 85 percent of accidents. If the other driver lacked liability insurance, compensation was received in only 25 percent of accidents (Committee to Study Compensation for Automobile Accidents, 1932, pp. 55–56). The study's authors concluded that a strict automobile-insurance plan modeled on recently enacted workers' compensation plans would address these issues. Each driver would be strictly liable to the other driver for whatever accidents were caused. Insurance would be required as a prerequisite to registering the vehicle (Y. Smith, Lilly, and Dowling, 1932, p. 798).

Noneconomic damages were excluded from the plan because it was modeled on contemporary workers' compensation plans and to constrain the costs of the new mandatory insurance (Y. Smith, Lilly, and Dowling, 1932, p. 802). Smith and colleagues, otherwise sympathetic reviewers of the plan, questioned the exclusion of noneconomic damages but noted that some limitation on damages was necessary to make the plan affordable to "the man of small means" (p. 802).

---

[13] There were a few important antecedents to the more widely publicized committee study. These include Ballantine (1916), Carman (1919), and Rollins (1919).

Critics of the report argued that it was suggesting "social and economic revolution," an especially weighty charge in the era (Lilly, 1932, p. 804). Austin Lilly also argued that the costs of the committee's plan would far surpass the optimistic estimates of its proponents. Those estimates were based on static models drawn from the past. Foreshadowing arguments that we hear today, Lilly said that malingering[14] and high medical costs[15] would drive up the costs of the no-fault system. Others argued that such a far-reaching scheme would be unconstitutional under both state and federal constitutions (Dowling, 1932, p. 813).

Some critics of the existing fault system suggested that the actual practice of insurance adjustment in automobile accidents was not really based on the principle of fault:

> The figures, however, themselves, demonstrate that the idea that the individual moral culpability is the basis for shifting losses is little more or less than a pious fraud . . . . The percentage of recovery, without inquiry as to fault, in insured fatal cases runs to 88% in insured cases of permanent disability to 96%. It is hardly conceivable that the line which fault would cleave in these instances runs at all in the neighborhood of these percentages. (Landis, 1932, pp. 1428–1429)

Landis argued that, rather than being a morally required prerequisite to liability, fault was a "pious fraud" that could easily be scrapped, since it was not, in practice, limiting liability in cases in which there was insurance.

---

[14] "The play allowed to neurasthenia, hypochondria, self-pity and the like, whether of the patient, if an adult, or of the parents if the patient be a child of tender years, in its effect upon compensated disability" (Lilly, 1932, p. 811).

[15] "The effect upon medical costs of permitting the claimants to select his or her own physician and to incur at someone else's expense, medical and hospital bills practically without limit; and, with due respect, the effect thereof upon the period of disability,—and this without the slightest necessary reflection upon the good faith of either patient or physician, except as they are of the race and subject to the influences which impinge upon all humanity" (Lilly, 1932, p. 811).

## As Automobile-Accident Costs Continue to Rise, More Studies Call for Variations on a No-Fault Approach to Auto Insurance: 1940–1970

In the 1950s and 1960s, there was a steady rise in the number and amount of automobile-related lawsuits. Between 1955 and 1970, the number of these lawsuits increased by 50 percent (Enzer, 1974, p. 88). Automobile-insurance liability premiums increased from $2.4 billion in 1955 to $8.9 billion in 1970 (Insurance Information Institute, 1976).

The steady growth in liability and lawsuits was caused by a number of factors. Increasing levels of car ownership, congestion, and density in the growth of cities led to more automobile accidents (Abraham, 2008, p. 82). Table 3.1 shows the steep growth in the number of cars and vehicle-miles traveled between 1945 and 1970.

The plaintiffs' trial bar also grew more sophisticated during this era. Melvin Belli, a central figure in the National Association of Claimants' Compensation Attorneys,[16] pioneered various methods of convincing a jury to return much higher verdicts for pain and suffering than had been common (Abraham, 2008, pp. 83–84). Because liability insurance became increasingly common, automobile-related personal-injury litigation became more lucrative for contingency fee–based plaintiffs' lawyers.

**Table 3.1**
**Number of Registered Automobiles and Passenger-Miles Traveled, 1945–1970**

| Travel Data | 1945 | 1950 | 1960 | 1970 |
|---|---|---|---|---|
| Number of registered automobiles (millions) | 26 | 41 | 62 | 89 |
| Annual passenger-car distance traveled in miles (billions) | 200 | 365 | 587 | 919 |

SOURCE: DOT (2003).

---

[16] This was the antecedent to the Association of Trial Lawyers of America, which is now called the American Association for Justice.

Overall and per capita medical costs also increased rapidly in this era, as is shown in Table 3.2.

This rapid increase in medical costs affected liability costs directly and indirectly. As injury victims received more-expensive care, they sought increased amounts from defendants to cover that care. It also affected liability costs indirectly through noneconomic damages. Non-economic damages were sometimes calculated by adjusters as a multiple of three or four times medical costs (Ross, 1980, pp. 109–110).[17] The increase in medical costs would then increase these noneconomic damages significantly.

The widespread growth of private first-party health insurance also led to an increase in the overall consumption of health care in the wake of an automobile accident. Automobile-accident victims would seek treatment, confident that they would recover their costs from their first-party insurance. This led to a general increase in the consumption of accident-related health care. Again, because noneconomic damages were sometimes informally calculated as a multiple of the medical damages, the increase in medical costs had a multiplier effect and increased damage amounts throughout the tort system (Abraham, 2008, pp. 85–87).

All of these factors led to growth in liability costs, and rising costs dominated policy discussions, sometimes leading to tumultuous public hearings. In Boston, for example, in 1955, insults and threats punc-

**Table 3.2**
**Growth in Health-Care Costs**

| Health-Care Expenditure | 1960 | 1970 | 1980 | 1990 | 2000 |
|---|---|---|---|---|---|
| Per capita (in current dollars) | 148 | 356 | 1,100 | 2,813 | 4,790 |
| As a proportion of gross domestic product (%) | 5.2 | 7.2 | 9.1 | 12.3 | 13.8 |

SOURCE: CMS (undated).

---

[17] Galanter (1996, pp. 1120–1123) notes that the ratio of noneconomic to economic loss has steadily declined over time, from 2.34 in 1977 to 1.87 in 1992, suggesting a "steady decline in the compensation for noneconomic loss."

tuated the annual insurance rate-setting hearing (*Boston Daily Globe*, 1955, p. 1). The focus on addressing the growth in number and size of claims left unaddressed the problems identified in the 1932 study by the Committee to Study Compensation for Automobile Accidents.

The committee's plan fared better elsewhere. In Canada, in 1946, Saskatchewan was the first jurisdiction to pass a no-fault automobile plan partially modeled on Columbia University's Committee to Study Compensation for Automobile Accidents (1932). All drivers were required to purchase first-party personal-injury loss insurance that would pay without respect to fault. The benefits were constrained by an injury schedule. Noneconomic damages (e.g., pain and suffering) were not compensable under the plan. Unlike the proposed Columbia plan, victims were permitted to recover in tort, subject to deduction of the benefits received under the loss insurance.[18] Drivers were required to purchase $35,000 liability coverage for amounts that exceeded the tort threshold. As R. Keeton and O'Connell (1965, p. 143) later noted, "under the Saskatchewan Plan no victim is worse off than under the old common law system, and some are substantially better off."[19]

In the United States, however, no jurisdiction had adopted meaningful reforms. In 1951, noted tort-law scholars Fleming James and Stewart Law conducted additional empirical research on automobile accidents in New Haven, Connecticut, and gloomily concluded that little progress had been made since the Columbia study: "the *same* facts and the *same* problems are still with us today" (James and Law, 1952, p. 81).

Over the next 30 years, proposals for no-fault explored different variations. For example, in 1954, Professor Albert A. Ehrenzweig published *"Full Aid" Insurance for the Traffic Victim*, proposing a system of

---

[18] Stat. Sask., ch. 38 § 32 (8) (a)-(b); § 69(1).

[19] In considering the relevance of Saskatchewan's experience to the United States, R. Keeton and O'Connell (1965, p. 146) argued that adding loss insurance on top of tort liability would make automobile insurance prohibitively expensive in many parts of the much more urbanized United States.

voluntary accident insurance without regard to fault or negligence.[20] If a driver purchased this new insurance, he or she "would be relieved from his common-law liability for ordinary . . . negligence" (Ehrenzweig, 1954, p. 30). Benefits would be paid on a third-party basis.[21] Benefits would not include compensation for pain and suffering and would be payable according to a schedule roughly comparable to those used under workers' compensation plans. To build on existing financial-responsibility laws, this insurance would require a driver to purchase it after his or her first accident (Ehrenzweig, 1954, p. 38). This plan garnered some interest, but it was criticized for not being fully developed (R. Keeton and O'Connell, 1965, p. 172).[22]

In 1958, a plan called for completely abolishing tort actions in automobile accidents. Leon Green, former dean of Northwestern University School of Law, published *Traffic Victims: Tort Law and Insurance*, proposing a form of no-fault loss insurance. Pain and suffering would not be compensated.

In 1962, professors Clarence Morris and James Paul proposed a plan that involved the then-novel use of monetary thresholds to determine whether compensation for pain and suffering would be permitted. They first conducted an empirical study and concluded that almost half of automobile-accident victims receive no compensation from insurance or their workplace (Morris and Paul, 1962, p. 933). They thought it futile to propose radical revisions of the existing system of liability law. Instead, they proposed an emergency fund that was available to victims only when other sources of recovery (e.g., health insurance and sick leave) fell "disastrously short of the tangible loss inflicted

---

[20] Ehrenzweig contrasted his "full aid" with the limited "first aid" provisions then found in some insurance policies (e.g., limited first-party MedPay insurance).

[21] There is, surprisingly, some ambiguity as to whether Ehrenzweig intended a first- or third-party plan (R. Keeton and O'Connell, 1965, p. 172).

[22] It is an interesting precursor of the choice approach, since it permitted individual drivers to opt out of the common-law liability system.

by the accident" (Morris and Paul, 1962, p. 926).[23] This fund would be financed by a variety of taxes.

To keep claims against the fund low, Morris and Paul (1962, p. 930) proposed treating claims below a particular threshold ($800) differently by (1) not permitting pain and suffering or claims of mental anguish, (2) offsetting the tort award by any benefits received from other sources,[24] and (3) requiring the defendant to pay for the claimant's attorney. This last provision was designed to make up for the fact that the other rules made these claims less attractive to attorneys.

Besides these specific calls for adopting some variation of a no-fault approach, other academic commentators attacked the centrality of fault. Some argued that fault itself actually hindered rehabilitation after an automobile accident:

> Too often the accident victim's own energies are directed toward retribution instead of restoration. In this misdirected effort, he may be encouraged by his family, his attorney, the adversary posture of the company involved or by his own bewilderment and frustration. (Henle, 1970, pp. 18–19)

---

[23] In 1964, Alfred Conard similarly found that many accident victims received no compensation at all from any source (Conard, 1964, p. 138). Conard collected data on the compensation systems of England, France, West Germany, and Sweden. He noted the widespread social-insurance safety net that meant that "health and medical expenses are so largely cared for without resort either to the patient's savings or to the liability of a tort-feasor" (p. 416).

[24] This would serve to abolish the traditional collateral-source rule. This is the rule that plaintiffs in personal-injury actions can recover full damages even if they have already received compensation for their injuries from another source. The conventional justification for this rule is that tortfeasors should not receive a windfall from injuring victims who had the foresight to secure insurance or disability benefits. Absent such a rule, it is thought that purchase of insurance might be reduced because purchasers might fear that whatever amounts recovered under the policy would be deducted from tort recoveries (*Arambula v. Wells*, 72 Cal. App. 4th 1006, 1999, in which the court explained the justification for the collateral-source rule). Other justifications for the collateral-source rule hinge on the existence of subrogation—if a court knows that the plaintiff is not going to get double recovery because his or her insurer will subrogate for the tort judgment, the question may become whether the defendant (or his or her insurer) or the plaintiff's insurer will ultimately bear the costs (Fleming, 1966, p. 1546).

Other writers argued that, whatever its merits in other settings, the notion of fault made little sense applied to most automobile accidents because the inattention that caused automobile accidents was inevitable (DOT, 1970, p. 100, quoting Norman, 1962, p. 51).

Not every academic accepted that the no-fault approach would inevitably be superior. The leading academic opponents of changes to the existing liability system were Walter Blum and Harry Kalven, who published *Public Law Perspectives on a Private Law Problem: Auto Compensation Plans* (1965). Blum and Kalven argued that the critics of the existing system of tort simply had not carried the burden necessary to undertake a radical change in the way in which automobile accidents were compensated. They opposed the fairness of ending compensation for pain and suffering, particularly for victims whose purely economic loss might be comparatively small because they were not in the workforce (e.g., spouses not employed outside the home, children) (Blum and Kalven, 1965, pp. 672–673). This was related to their skepticism toward the loss-spreading function of tort law. In their view, tort law's primary function was corrective justice. Distributive-justice issues—such as ensuring adequate compensation for those injured in automobile accidents—should be addressed by the Social Security system or another government program that would apply to all accident victims and not just those injured by an auto (Blum and Kalven, 1973).

Blum and Kalven were also very skeptical of predictions of massive cost savings from the reduction of administrative costs. They argued that, since no-fault automobile-insurance plans cover more victims, they will almost certainly be more expensive than tort systems:

> To accomplish the extension of coverage, a plan must change the allocation of costs generally. Stated simply, the money for the newly covered victims must come from somewhere. (Blum and Kalven, 1964, p. 669)

They also feared that fraud would inflate costs (Blum and Kalven, 1964, p. 683) and that the lack of scrutiny of claims would increase both the volume of claims and the likelihood of fraud (Blum and Kalven, 1964, p. 689). These concerns would prove prophetic.[25]

Despite Blum and Kalven's skepticism, other early estimates of cost savings for no-fault were substantial. In 1968, the American Insurance Association modeled the cost of no-fault on a set of 11,000 personal-injury accidents collected over several weeks. They found that consumers purchasing no-fault insurance would save 29 percent (King, 1968, p. 1163).

In this era, there were some limited no-fault experiments in the United States. In 1968, several insurance companies pilot-tested a postaccident elective no-fault insurance system in several counties in New York (King, 1968, pp. 1152–1158). This experiment allowed accident victims to forgo tort recoveries in return for increased disability payments. Similarly, Nationwide Mutual Insurance Company had uniquely offered a first-party insurance plan to those it insured for approximately a decade but found the results disappointing (King, 1968, p. 1157). A number of other plans were proposed, but none was enacted.[26]

---

[25] Later, Blum and Kalven (1973) noted that the shift from third-party to first-party insurance could have large regressive effects. Higher-income insureds would have larger claims because no-fault insurance covered lost wages. Since charging higher-wage insureds higher premiums was not feasible, the result would be a subsidy of higher-income insureds by lower-income insureds.

[26] These included the 1968 plan by the American Insurance Association, the 1970 plan by the National Association of Independent Insurers, and a 1972 plan by the National Conference of Commissioners on Uniform State Laws. One interesting plan that was proposed by Bradford Smith, chair of Insurance Company of North America, was direct coverage with subrogation. Under this plan, the insured could voluntarily elect to relinquish benefits from collateral sources and reduce his or her premium. After an accident, the insurer would provide first-party benefits to the insured but then seek compensation against any third parties who might be found liable under traditional tort doctrine. A victim is free to sue for pain and suffering but cannot refer to the "specials" for which he or she has already received compensation—a practical impediment to recovering pain and suffering (King, 1968, pp. 1158–1159).

## Massachusetts Becomes the First State to Adopt No-Fault: 1965–1970

In 1965, professors Robert Keeton and Jeffrey O'Connell published *Basic Protection for the Traffic Victim: A Blueprint for Reforming Automobile Insurance*. In this landmark work, they chronicled "shortcomings of the present system" (R. Keeton and O'Connell, 1965, p. 1).

Keeton and O'Connell (1965, pp. 2–3) focused generally on five problems:

> (1) As a result of the fault standard, many victims were either not compensated at all or undercompensated. (2) There was a long delay in providing compensation to injured persons. (3) The seriously injured were often undercompensated, while victims with minor injuries are often overcompensated. (4) The process of establishing fault creates high administrative costs. (5) Victims and injurers have large incentives to be dishonest in their attempts to improve their cases.

These concerns were very similar to those that drove the authors of the Columbia plan 40 years earlier.

More generally, Keeton and O'Connell (1965, p. 21) attacked the idea of fault itself applied to automobile accidents and argued that "fault is an unrealistic criterion" for assigning the cost of accidents. They also captured the nation's divided attitudes about driving:

> You are told that they kill almost 50,000 people annually and injure millions more. And in the next moment you are exhorted to cast inhibition to the winds—to "put a tiger in your tank" and drive a car named "Fury," "Wildcat," or "Marauder" (which means literally one who pillages and lays waste to the countryside!) Who can be surprised, then that notions of individual fault in traffic accidents are confused and blurred? (Keeton and O'Connell, 1965, p. 22)

To address these problems, they proposed a detailed plan for first-party insurance to replace third-party liability and third-party liability insurance. Instead of suing the negligent injurer and hoping that one could prove negligence, a victim would simply recover from his or her own insurer without respect to negligence. Cost savings would come from the reduction in administrative costs and the fact that pain and suffering would not be covered by the first-party insurance.

Why exclude pain and suffering, which are historically considered important components of compensation? Blum and Kalven (1973, p. 346) cite (1) a desire to keep damage assessment as objective as possible to maximize administrative efficiency, (2) the sense that some items of common-law damages are simply "unsound," (3) "a distaste for the exploitation felt to be involved in the publicized million dollar awards," and (4) that having a plan quite so expensive would be "impolitic." They also suggest that automobile no-fault demonstrates a philosophical shift away from the traditional corrective-justice function of tort law toward an insurance-compensation rationale (Blum and Kalven, 1973, p. 346).

Keeton and O'Connell were well aware of the fates of the many previous no-fault plans. To avoid similar irrelevance, they included a detailed draft statute and a formal actuarial opinion that the plan would save money.[27]

One of Keeton's former students, Michael Dukakis, had firsthand experience with litigating accident cases and was appalled by the level of fraud and abuse that the tort system for auto cases entailed. In conjunction with Keeton, Dukakis drafted a no-fault bill and was able to pass it, over the opposition of trial lawyers and the insurance industry, in Massachusetts (Burke, 2002, p. 107). It went into effect January 1, 1971.[28]

---

[27] O'Connell believes that both of these factors—unusual accompaniments to a law-review article—were critical to the subsequent passage of the bill. O'Connell credits Keeton with the idea of including a statute (O'Connell, 2008).

[28] Puerto Rico had introduced a no-fault system in 1969 (Oliphant, 2007, p. 52).

### Insurance Industry Divides Over No-Fault

Prior to the 1970s, the insurance industry had generally opposed mandatory no-fault insurance and, indeed, mandatory insurance of any kind. This opposition stemmed from concern about changing their successful business model and, more specifically, concern about the regulatory oversight that laws requiring insurance would likely bring.[29]

The insurance industry did not have a uniform position on no-fault laws during the early 1970s. Some insurers believed that ever-climbing tort costs and increasingly aggressive plaintiffs' lawyers required a radical new approach. Other insurers were concerned that large PIP coverage with ineffectual tort limitations might actually drive up premium costs and increase pressure on regulators to reduce insurer profits (Harrington, 1994, p. 280).

In the early 1970s, State Farm Insurance's first general counsel, Donald McHugh, saw the potential benefits of no-fault and convinced State Farm to support it. This support would last roughly for the next 25 years. Travelers Insurance also supported no-fault until around 2002. Similarly, United Services Automobile Association actively supported no-fault during this period.[30] In an era of sharply rising auto-insurance premium costs, no-fault was also seen as preferable to other reform efforts—including more-direct regulation of rates by the states.

Other insurers, including Allstate, opposed it. While the promise of reducing tort costs was attractive, the insurers perceived that their expertise was in actuarially rating the costs of common accidents and the subsequent litigation. Anything that threatened that pattern also threatened the insurers' fundamental business model (O'Connell, 2008).

Keeton and O'Connell thought that, from a policy perspective, the ideal no-fault law is one that provides large or unlimited benefits in the very small subset of catastrophic accidents and nothing in the vast majority of automobile accidents without serious injury. From a loss-spreading perspective, this seemed desirable: It provided compensation

---

[29] For examples of insurance-company opposition to no-fault approaches, see Hensley (1962), Knepper (1962), Kramer (1959), and Sherman (1936).

[30] Based on author interview with not-for-attribution insurer sources.

to those who most needed it and nothing to those whose losses were not serious. This was, not surprisingly, anathema to lawyers for whom numerous small automobile-accident claims made up a substantial proportion of their business.

Interestingly, many insurers also resisted this vision because, actuarially, small frequent claims are much easier to predict (and derive rates for) than larger, much less frequent claims (O'Connell, 2008). This is simply a function of the law of large numbers (Tijms, 2007, p. 17). It was not only more difficult to predict the frequency of large claims; it was also more difficult to predict their exact size, because the size of the claim depended on many individual factors that did not occur frequently enough to generate reliable actuarial estimates. Thus, there was a conflict between what seemed actuarially attractive to insurers and what seemed desirable to reformers, as a policy matter. Some insurers, therefore, felt that it was in their financial interest to maintain the status quo instead of moving to a system that focused on compensating victims for large losses (O'Connell, 2008).

Originally, Keeton and O'Connell envisioned no-fault auto insurance (PIP) as secondary to the victim's health insurance. Victims would initially recover from their health insurance before seeking compensation for any uncovered costs from their auto insurer. Auto insurers, however, were concerned that such a no-fault regime would dramatically reduce premiums and potentially vastly reduce their business. If auto accident–related medical costs were being paid through health insurance rather than auto insurance, much of auto insurance might be swallowed up by first-party medical insurance. As a result, auto insurers pushed for auto insurance to be the primary payer in Massachusetts and in subsequent no-fault bills in other states (O'Connell, 2008).[31]

Publicly, auto insurers argued that the costs of automobile accidents should be internalized to that activity. If society allows health insurance to pay the costs of automobile accidents, then, they argued,

---

[31] Today, Michigan and New Jersey permit the insured to choose to make auto insurance secondary to first-party medical insurance.

people will drive too much, because the costs of driving will not be internalized to that activity (O'Connell, 2008).[32]

No-fault supporters were critical of this argument. Some viewed automobile accidents as caused by momentary lapses of attention that were more or less randomly distributed. The very idea that automobile accidents were anyone's fault, in this view, was essentially a counter-productive fiction that needlessly complicated the process of compensating the injured (see, e.g., Rokes, 1971; R. Keeton and O'Connell, 1965, p. 16). A 1970 U.S. Department of Transportation study suggested that automobile accidents are unresponsive to tort incentives because they are randomly distributed among the driving population (DOT, 1970).[33] Hence, attempts to place the costs of automobile accidents on unsafe drivers would be futile.[34]

In any event, the effect of the decision to make auto insurance the primary payer rather than first-party medical insurance was long lasting. It meant that a no-fault regime would shift costs away from first-party medical insurers to the no-fault automobile-insurance system. As we explain in Chapter Five, these medical costs are primarily responsible for the rise in the cost of no-fault.

## Rise of No-Fault and Consumer Rights: 1970–1985

In the early to mid-1970s, no-fault was seriously considered in many states. While there were state-by-state variations, depending on the local political terrain, in general, consumer advocates and academics supported some form of no-fault. The consumer movement was developing into a distinct political force in the era, and no-fault automobile insurance seemed to be a clearly superior policy innovation. O'Connell,

---

[32] In theory, when pricing premiums on an individual basis, health insurers could take into account all the facts that auto insurers consider, but this would be a dramatic change from the group pricing that is typically used in pricing health insurance.

[33] We discuss the incentive effects of automobile insurance regimes in Chapter Five.

[34] See, e.g., Kozyris (1972, p. 331): The traditional tort approach is "anachronistic because it is based upon fault principles when it is becoming increasingly apparent that a large proportion of accidents are due to the inherent risks of driving rather than individual fault."

coauthor of the 1965 proposal, recalls being met at airports by television crews prior to testifying at public hearings on the advantages of the no-fault system. The evening news would then feature his comments on the advantages of no-fault insurance, and further political pressure would build for this reform (Abraham, 2008, p. 96). Similarly, Senator Daniel Moynihan called no-fault "the one incontestably successful reform of the 1960s" (O'Connell, 1975, pp. x–xi).[35]

Figure 3.1 shows the rapid spread of no-fault laws in the early 1970s. Between 1970 and 1976, 26 states passed some form of no-fault insurance requirement.

In New York, for example, Governor Nelson Rockefeller appointed the Governor's Committee on Compensating Victims of Automobile Accidents.[36] The committee's report concluded that the existing system does a very poor job of allocating the costs of automobile accidents. The report chronicles the by now–familiar list of criticisms of the fault system, including the following:

- *uncompensated victims:* Many victims receive no compensation at all from the fault insurance system (Stewart, 1970, p. 18).
- *delay:* The system takes too long to provide compensation when it does so (Stewart, 1970, pp. 19–20).
- *disproportionate benefits:* Benefits are not proportionate to the seriousness of the injuries.
- *no coordination of benefits:* Because of the collateral-source rule, tort insurance benefits are not coordinated with other sources.
- *rehabilitation hindered:* In the most serious of injuries, the fault system's delays in payments hinder necessary rehabilitation.
- *unnecessary costs:* Administrative and legal costs use $0.56 out of every premium dollar.

---

[35] Indeed, flush from the victory in the statehouses, O'Connell (1975) proposed extending a form of no-fault coverage to products and services.

[36] The fact that the governor's report opens with an excerpt from Franz Kafka's (1956) *The Trial* gives the reader a sense of the authors' regard for the existing system of compensating automobile-accident victims.

**Figure 3.1
Automobile-Insurance Regimes, by State and Year**

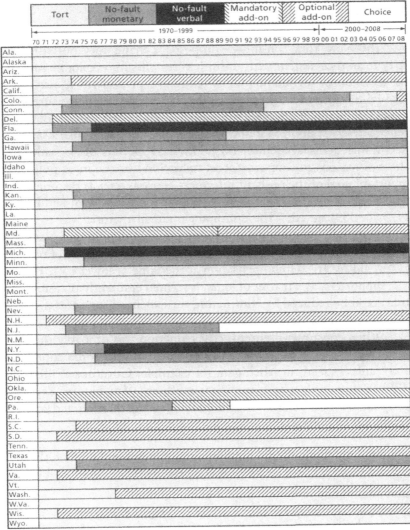

RAND *MG860-3.1*

- *fostering dishonesty:* The fault system encourages dishonesty by both claimants and insurers.
- *overall costs:* Overall premium rates are very high and continue to rise (Stewart, 1970).

The New York committee proposed a mandatory no-fault first-party insurance system with unlimited benefits for economic loss and the abolition of tort claims for all cases except death.[37] It also had a "bad-faith" provision, imposing "heavy sanctions" on insurers for unfair treatment of claimants (Stewart, 1970, p. 98). Governor Rockefeller actively supported it and was able to get it passed in 1972.[38]

While many academic and political supporters of no-fault cited a host of reasons to support it, cost reduction was the most politically important goal of the no-fault reformers and was seen as the one of the most effective means of mobilizing support for it. As Blum and Kalven (1973, p. 359) noted, "The dominant political rhetoric was to promise virtually all motorists an actual reduction in premiums." Similarly, O'Connell and Joost (1986) later explained that the promise of no-fault was providing greater compensation at the same or lower cost. For no-fault supporters, as a matter of logic, it seemed eminently plausible that costs could be reduced by eliminating the expensive, unnecessary legal apparatus of apportioning fault.

While consumer-premium cost reduction was probably the most politically salient goal, it was only one of many to some supporters of no-fault. Indeed, in Michigan, for example, Governor William G. Milliken and insurance commissioner Russell Van Hooser explicitly *deemphasized* cost reduction as a goal. Instead, they offered a much broader set of purposes:

(1) Compensate injured persons adequately, promptly, and without regard to fault for medical expenses, wage loss, or rehabilita-

---

[37] Interestingly, it required motorists to purchase the insurance unless it was less expensive to purchase health or wage-loss insurance to provide the primary coverage (Stewart, 1970, pp. 89–90). Thus, in this plan, there was no necessity that the auto insurance be the primary source of indemnity.

[38] New York's current no-fault law is codified at N.Y. Ins. Law 5101.

tion expenses. (2) Reduce or eliminate the nuisance value of small claims. (3) Reduce the duplication and overlapping of benefits within the auto-insurance system and other systems. If the duplication is not reduced or eliminated, it should at least be subject to greater consumer control so that the consumer will have a corresponding control over his or her costs. (4) Reduce or eliminate of some of the other frictions and inefficiencies of the present system, such as the adversarial relationship between insured and injured party, court congestion, litigation expense, and overhead expense. (Jones, 1977, p. 381)

But this deemphasis of cost was the exception rather than the rule. While policymakers may have been interested in wider effects of no-fault, cost reduction was the most salient issue for most voters and legislators. Indeed, a rise in premium costs was often the impetus for politicians to consider no-fault in the first place (Lascher, 1999, pp. 28–35).[39]

No-fault was part of a wave of consumer-oriented reforms and doctrinal changes that swept the tort system. These included expansion of the scope of duty in negligence law, reduction of tort immunities, expansion of vicarious liability, adoption of comparative negligence, market-share theories of causation, extension of liability to successor corporations, and extension of dram-shop liability (Rahdert, 1995, pp. 75–76).[40]

In the legal academy, Guido Calabresi published *The Costs of Accidents* in 1970, which was generally critical of using the fault standard to allocate liability. In other articles, he influentially argued for strict-liability approaches (that is, liability without fault) to tort (Calabresi and Hirschoff, 1972). Similarly, Congress passed the Magnuson-Moss Warranty Act (Pub. L. 93-637) in 1975 that expanded consumer rights

---

[39] Harrington's (1994) regression analysis showed that the probability of adopting no-fault was higher in states with more-rapid growth in insurance costs.

[40] Dram-shop liability is liability that a bar or restaurant has for injuries that are caused by the business's intoxicated customers. Typically, when this doctrine of dram-shop liability is invoked, victims of automobile accidents that involved alcohol allege that a bar continued to serve an intoxicated patron.

with respect to warranties. All of these developments were championed by the plaintiffs' bar because they expanded consumer rights, gave consumers more causes of action, or narrowed defenses.

No-fault, in contrast, was the rare, consumer-oriented tort reform that *narrowed* the consumer's ability to sue. While it was supported by a coalition of some consumer groups, good-government politicians, and academics, plaintiffs' lawyers strongly and consistently opposed it.[41] They argued that no-fault wrongly deprived an injured plaintiff of his or her right to a day in court and that the noneconomic damages that no-fault sought to eliminate, such as pain and suffering, were important and should be compensable, particularly for those who suffered little economic damage.[42]

## Evaluations of No-Fault Were Generally Positive but Noted Higher-Than-Expected Premium Costs

Early evaluations of no-fault regimes were generally positive and found that such regimes were successful in accomplishing many of their goals. Even these early studies noted, however, that costs were higher than anticipated. For example, in 1977, Alan Widiss and others published a study of the no-fault experience to date, looking at Massachusetts, Florida, Delaware (a mandatory–add-on state), and Michigan. In Massachusetts, he found that PIP claimants were generally happy:

> [T]he industry sought to use the introduction of no-fault insurance as a means of substantially improving its relationships with consumers in Massachusetts. The survey data . . . demonstrate, that from the perspective of the PIP claimant, the industry has

---

[41] The American Bar Association (ABA) Section of Negligence, Insurance and Compensation Law opposed no-fault because "the principle of liability for fault is derived from the religious belief that each of us is responsible to his God for his own conduct" ("The Drama with a Case of 100 Million," 1968). The fact that a section of the ABA opposed no-fault suggests that many defense lawyers also opposed it (Peck, 2009).

[42] The risk of a national no-fault bill prompted the Association of Trial Lawyers of America to open a Washington, D.C., office for the first time (Burke, 2002, p. 109).

made significant progress towards this goal. (Widiss et al., 1977, p. 79)

Prior to the introduction of no-fault, 78 percent of Massachusetts victims retained lawyers (DOT, 1970, p. 78).[43] After the passage of no-fault, in 1970, many lawyers refused to handle PIP claims and advised prospective clients to file the PIP claims themselves, although some lawyers did take those cases (Widiss et al., 1977, p. 97). Widiss and his coauthors concluded that the vast majority of victims who filed only PIP claims represented themselves. After no-fault, attorneys represented only about 50 percent of liability claimants, mostly in connection with third-party tort claims for cases in which the threshold was exceeded (Widiss et al., 1977, p. 99).

The vast majority of lawyers indicated that no-fault had little effect on their practice. Only about one-sixth reported that the advent of no-fault significantly affected their practice (Widiss et al., 1977, p. 107).[44] Interestingly, Widiss found the attitudes of the bar divided. The majority felt that there was no need for a lawyer's assistance in filling out a PIP claim,[45] but a substantial minority disagreed. One such lawyer explained, "you always need an attorney when an insurance company is involved" (Widiss et al., 1977, p. 101). This was not the attitude that the proponents of no-fault insurance hoped would emerge. One of the prime arguments in favor of no-fault is that it would eliminate the litigation and contentiousness associated with compensation for automobile accidents.

Widiss also observed that most attorneys felt that getting involved in suing a first-party insurance company was rarely worthwhile because the amounts in question were always very small (Widiss et al., 1977, p. 103). This contrasts with the later rise of first-party bad-faith lawsuits.

---

[43] The 78-percent representation figure was higher than for any other state surveyed.

[44] In Massachusetts, concerns about the constitutionality of the limitation on pain and suffering were not resolved until the Massachusetts Supreme Court decided *Pinnick v. Cleary*, 360 Mass. 1 (1971).

[45] "It's just like Blue Cross or any health or accident claim," explained one lawyer who thought that consulting an attorney was unnecessary for PIP claims (Widiss et al., 1977, p. 100).

Initially, no-fault's effect on filings was dramatic. In one large county, BI claims from motor-vehicle accidents fell by 93 percent (Widiss et al., 1977, p. 117). This is somewhat surprising, because the threshold to reach tort and recover for pain and suffering was only $500 ($2,219 in 2000 inflation-adjusted dollars) under the Massachusetts statute.

Unexpectedly, property-damage (PD) claims also dropped dramatically in Massachusetts following the passage of no-fault. Apparently, many PD claims that were too small to stand alone were often included in BI claims. Once most BI claims were moved to the first-party system, the add-on PD claims also disappeared (Widiss et al., 1977, p. 145). Reviews of the Florida and Michigan systems were similarly positive. In short, it appeared as though no-fault functioned as intended—reducing costs and moving smaller claims out of the tort system.

Not all reviews were quite so positive. In Delaware, a review after the first two years of add-on found that there was little or no reduction in cases filed (Clark and Waterson, 1974, p. 231). As might be expected under an add-on system, the number of BI claims dropped, but the overall claim activity rose (Clark and Waterson, 1974, p. 253).

In 1985, the U.S. Department of Transportation published its own report on the no-fault experiment. On every metric except cost, it gave no-fault glowing marks:

> More victims receive compensation under no-fault than under fault systems. The number of paid claims per 100 insured cars averages 1.8 under PIP in the 22 no-fault states as compared to 0.9 for BI liability insurance in 28 traditional states.

> Under no-fault, victims have access to greater amount of money. No-fault states require on average $15,000 in PIP coverage in addition to liability coverage.

> Compensation under no-fault occurs far more swiftly than fault states. Within one year, PIP claimants had received 99.5% of the total money they were due. In contrast, BI liability claimants had

received only 51.7% of the total money they would receive within one year.

Claimants receive a higher proportion of premium payments under no-fault. Under no-fault, average claimant received 50.2 cents compared to average fault state returned 43.2 cents.

No-fault states had proportionately fewer lawsuits than fault states.

Both no-fault and fault provide insufficient benefits for the catastrophically injured.

No-fault does not lead to additional accidents. (DOT, 1985, pp. 3–6)

The report noted, however, that no-fault states have higher overall insurance costs and that "expenses in no-fault states are increasing faster than expenses in fault states" (DOT, 1985, pp. 3–6). The report also noted that the average motorist regards cost as the only important criterion of effectiveness (DOT, 1985, p. 67).

The unexpectedly high costs of no-fault were recognized as a problem. O'Connell and Joost (1986, p. 62) noted that "the original proponents of no-fault automobile insurance promised that it would provide greater compensation to accident victims at the same or lower cost than traditional tort-based liability insurance." Yet, they noted that the cost of no-fault insurance in some states has been unexpectedly high.

In response to the controversy engendered by the costs and mandatory nature of the existing no-fault plans, O'Connell and Joost proposed a "choice" no-fault plan in their 1986 article. This proposition would permit each auto-insurance consumer to choose between a no-fault plan, in which he or she would give up some of his or her tort rights, in exchange for premium savings or retaining the conventional right to sue.[46]

---

[46] O'Connell and Joost (1986, p. 82) explained the consumer to whom each approach might appeal:

John Rolph conducted a study in 1985 for the RAND Institute for Civil Justice that also generally gave the no-fault system good marks. He concluded that victims in no-fault states collect more and that there was more consistency in payments than in tort states. He estimated that, in tort states, 20 percent of victims are not paid from any source, compared to only 13 percent in no-fault states (Rolph et al., 1985, p. 30).

Carroll, Kakalik, et al. (1991) conducted a more comprehensive analysis of the effect of no-fault. They concluded that no-fault plans reduced the gap between compensation and economic loss and that they reduced transaction costs, but by a limited amount. Whether or not no-fault reduced overall costs depended on the threshold and how generous PIP benefits were.

To sum up, no-fault was designed to address numerous problems that arose from using the tort system to compensate victims of automobile accidents. While the trial bar consistently opposed the reform, a variety of academics, consumer groups, and insurers sup-

---

The liability option might be a "better deal" than the no-fault option for individuals who have very high limits of both health insurance and income continuation insurance. It might also be preferred by individuals who view auto accidents as opportunities to "win" a large sum of money, rather than as misfortunes that can result in permanent injury, and who believe that there is no real danger of losing, because Medicare, Medicaid, and welfare will provide for them if they do not win a liability award. . . . The liability option would pay relatively more money than the no-fault option if the accident victim involved is one who has suffered only moderate injuries, such as back strain, whiplash or fracture. Moderate injuries can cause a great deal of pain and suffering, compensable under liability insurance but not under no-fault insurance.

In contrast, they wrote, no-fault would appeal to consumers

who want to be sure that catastrophic losses will not outstrip their own coverages no matter how high. It would certainly be better for individuals who do not have very high limits of both health insurance and income continuation insurance. It would also be the preferred choice of motorists who do not want to be paid for their pain and suffering but who do want swift, sure, and complete payment of their accident-caused personal economic losses. This option would be more attractive to people who dislike gambling, who eschew litigation, or who distrust lawyers. (O'Connell and Joost, 1986, p. 83)

In this way, the authors hoped to provide a politically viable plan that would retain most of the advantages of no-fault without requiring a jurisdiction-wide choice to adopt it.

ported it as a logical alternative to the excesses of the tort system. Early empirical evaluations indicated that it was largely accomplishing its multifaceted goals but that it remained more expensive than expected.

While this expense might have been a minor setback to no-fault proponents if there was widespread support for the many objectives of no-fault, this was not the case. Premium cost was easily the most important factor and the one that generated political pressure for legislatures to consider changing the automobile-insurance system (Harrington, 1994; Lascher, 1999, pp. 28–29). As Lascher observed (1999, p. 29), "it is not difficult to see why the public's concern was focused on rates rather than, say the adequacy or timeliness of benefits. Rate increases readily manifest themselves in highly visible, quantifiable measures." In every jurisdiction that Lascher (1999, p. 30) surveyed, "rate concerns were dominant, or the insurance issue tended to be off the agenda for elected officials."

## The California Experience with No-Fault

We consider the California experience with no-fault because it illustrates the shifting political debate over no-fault. At first, it appeared as though insurers and consumer advocates would convince proposition voters to enact no-fault. But its political opponents, primarily plaintiffs' lawyers, were able to defeat it by focusing the debate on premium costs and distrust of insurance companies. Today, many national insurers cite the California experience in explaining their tepid support of or opposition to no-fault systems.

In the 1980s in California, auto-insurance costs were an important political issue. Rates under the tort system had increased approximately 12 percent each year between 1982 and 1986, and many drivers were electing to drive without insurance at all (Zycher, 1990, p. 68). California had the fourth-highest insurance rates in the country, and there was some evidence that the high cost of insurance was leading to a vicious cycle as drivers dropped out of the insurance pool (Burke,

2002, p. 115). This was occurring against a backdrop of concern about the tort system and its apparently spiraling costs.

In the wake of a defeat over a limitation on joint and several liability for pain and suffering, California trial lawyers sought to meet with their adversaries to see whether there was room for compromise. After a series of discussions conducted by then–state senator Bill Lockyer and Speaker Willie Brown, the parties agreed to support a civil-liability reform bill that would raise statutory limits on fees but also make it harder to obtain punitive damages. The groups also agreed not to push for any legislation or propositions, including no-fault, for five years without consulting one another. Lockyer reputedly drafted a loose agreement on the back of a napkin, and the agreement was thereafter known as "the Napkin Deal at Frank Fat's," named for the Chinese restaurant in Sacramento where the meetings were held. Purportedly, the next *day*, September 11, 1987, the agreed-upon bill was passed by large margins in both houses (Burke, 2002, p. 111).

Consumer groups were furious at being excluded from the deal. For them, the Napkin Deal had the hallmarks of corruption. Moreover, consumer groups were disappointed that their traditional allies, the plaintiffs' lawyers, had made several concessions without any consultation with them. Harvey Rosenfield, a Ralph Nader–trained consumer activist, led the nonprofit organization Access to Justice and was one of the many consumer advocates unhappy with the Napkin Deal. Shortly after the truce on further propositions was announced, he announced that Access to Justice would press for a ballot initiative to increase the regulation of automobile insurance and lower automobile-insurance rates by 20 percent.

This development prompted much reaction. Breaking the truce of the Napkin Deal, insurers responded by drafting Proposition 104, a competing proposition to institute a no-fault auto-insurance system in California as an alternative way to control automobile-insurance costs. Unhappy with the breaching of the Napkin Deal truce, the California Trial Lawyers' Association (CTLA; now Consumer Attorneys of California) offered Proposition 100, calling for reducing premiums, requiring a good-driver discount, further regulating insurance rates, and prohibiting contingency-fee limitations. Another insurance group and a state legislator offered their own compromise proposal, and the insurers supporting no-fault offered another proposal as well. Five separate ballot initiatives concerning auto insurance were on the ballot in 1988 (Burke, 2002, pp. 112–114).

The no-fault plan advocated by the insurers required all drivers to insure themselves for $10,000 in medical expenses, $15,000 in wage losses, and $5,000 in funeral benefits. Claims for pain and suffering would be permitted only if injuries were "serious and permanent." This would be the strictest verbal threshold in the country. In return for these limitations, the bill guaranteed 20-percent reductions in BI, UIM, and MedPay portions of the policy.

Insurers spent more than $55 million to conduct a sophisticated media campaign to support the proposition. The CTLA spent $16 million. Nader, Rosenfield, and Access to Justice, with just $3 million, relied more on free media coverage. They used the amounts spent by the insurers and the proposition's complexity as key arguments for voters to oppose it. Consumer groups were successfully able to use the insurer's support for the measure as a reason that it should be opposed (Burke, 2002, 117). The insurers' no-fault initiative, Proposition 104, and the trial lawyers' Proposition 100 ultimately failed. Access to Justice's anti-insurer Proposition 103 was the only one that passed. But its central provision—an immediate 20-percent rollback on rates—was held unconstitutional by the California Supreme Court (*Calfarm Ins. Co. v. Deukmejian*, 771 P.2d 1247, Cal. 1989).

In the wake of Proposition 103, Democratic assemblymember Patrick Johnston and Consumers Union advocate Judith Bell both believed that no-fault had not received a careful evaluation by the voters and remained the key to lower automobile-insurance costs in the long run. While Consumers Union supported Proposition 103, it still felt that controlling the underlying costs of auto insurance was important. Johnston and Consumers Union had opposed the insurers' no-fault proposal, Proposition 104, because of its many additional provisions. But Consumers Union had long supported no-fault insurance as being a sensible reform that would aid consumers in receiving speedy, fair compensation for their injuries (Bell, 1988).

Johnston and Consumers Union planned to introduce a no-fault bill that was modeled after the New York no-fault system, generally considered successful in holding down costs. Drivers were required to carry $50,000 in PIP and $3,000 in funeral costs. The statute included a $50,000 monetary threshold that had to be crossed in order to reach the tort system. Proponents claimed that it would remove 80 percent of auto cases from the tort system (Hoffman, 1989).

Around the same time, two groups that focused on minority issues, Latino Issues Forum and Public Advocates, coalesced around a no-fault proposal. These groups were motivated by the regressive character of most automobile insurance and the effect that rising rates were having on minority communities. Because automobile insurance is priced according to territory, auto insurance in urban areas is much more expensive than auto insurance in suburban and more-rural areas. Density leads to more accidents and higher insurance rates.[47] Conventional tort was regressive in another way. Conventional tort-liability insurance rates necessarily included the cost of compensating for lost wages for the average wage earner. In contrast, a first-party policy sold to low-income drivers could be less expensive because it needed to cover only the cost of compensating the below-average income of these customers.

These higher rates were levied against those who were least able to afford them. A 1995 U.S. Department of Labor report estimated that the poorest quintile of Americans spent 4.3 percent of their total household income on auto insurance.[48] The proportion is even higher for the urban poor. Relatively poor public transportation to the suburbs—the location of many low-skill jobs—made matters worse. Finally, most of the driving poor were essentially judgment-proof. Owning insurance only helped the other driver. A poor person living in central Los Angeles faced a difficult choice: Pay a substantial proportion of one's

---

[47] Some have argued that this can create a vicious cycle because it leads to more drivers being unable to afford automobile insurance and electing to go without. The high prevalence of uninsured drivers simply increases insurance costs in the territory which in turn leads to more drivers dropping out of the pool. See Smith and Wright, 1992.

[48] See also O'Connell (1995, p. 41), who discusses a study that found that a low-income family would have to spend 30 percent of its income on liability insurance.

total income on auto insurance that provided little benefit to oneself, or simply drive illegally. Unsurprisingly, this led many poor urbanites, including Latinos and African Americans, to simply go without auto insurance and thereby violate the law (Burke, 2002, p. 120).

Public Advocates also believed that the right to sue that was venerated by the plaintiffs' attorneys, Ralph Nader, and other no-fault opponents was not worth as much for poor and minority groups. Lawyers willing to represent the very poor were harder to find. Lost wages were much lower, and jurors were less likely to return large awards.[49] Knowing that the poor lacked health insurance and needed immediate payment for medical bills, insurers could negotiate with them aggressively.

These reasons led Public Advocates and Latino Issues Forum to support a no-frills choice no-fault plan for a flat $160 anywhere in the state. Buyers would give up the right to sue for pain and suffering except in cases of serious and permanent injuries.

Johnston, Consumers Union, Latino Issues Forum, and Public Advocates jointly merged their separate proposals to create a broad coalition of support. This included the Western Division of the National Association for the Advancement of Colored People (NAACP), the American GI Forum, the California Council of Urban Leagues, the Mexican American Political Association, the Rainbow Coalition, the Black Business Association of Los Angeles, Chinese for Affirmative Action, the Filipino American Political Association, and some insurance companies, which were still hesitant after the proposition debacle (Reich, 1989a).

Against this broad coalition were the CTLA, Ralph Nader, and Harvey Rosenfield, the chief proponent of Proposition 103. Nader and Rosenfield argued that the coalition of minority groups was being used by the insurance industry. They argued that the choice plan designed for the poor would create a "two-class insurance system" that would unfairly deprive the poor of their right to be fully compen-

---

[49] Conventional tort liability insurance rates necessarily included the cost of compensating for lost wages for the average wage-earner. In contrast, a first-party policy sold to low-income drivers could be less expensive because it needed only to cover the cost of compensating the below-average income of the customers.

sated for pain and suffering. This, they argued, dehumanized the poor and deprived them of their equal rights (Reich, 1989b). The split in the left-leaning interest groups occasioned by no-fault—Ralph Nader and the trial lawyers on one side against Consumers Union, minority groups, and insurers on the other—shows the strange bedfellows that the debate over no-fault created.

Yet, despite the broad coalition that supported "no-frills no-fault," the CTLA was narrowly able to prevent it and its successors from passing in both 1989 and 1990. In each case, they were able to take advantage of the unpopularity of insurers and argue that the insurers were using the consumer groups as unwitting dupes to deprive people of their right to recover full compensation for their losses.

Despite these defeats, no-fault advocates continued to press for this reform. Financial columnist Andrew Tobias led an unsuccessful effort to convert California into $0.25-per-gallon gasoline tax–funded no-fault automobile-insurance system in 1993. The no-fault PIP would pay only for otherwise unreimbursed medical costs. This was opposed by insurers, insurance agents (who would lose commissions), oil companies (who feared the reduction in demand that an increase in net gasoline price might cause), rural motorists (who drove long distances), and plaintiffs' lawyers (who opposed any no-fault system).[50]

Finally, in 1996, a coalition of Silicon Valley high-tech companies supported Proposition 200 (Pure No-Fault Auto Insurance Act), a pure no-fault system that barred almost all lawsuits. Once again, consumer groups were split, with Consumers Union, key supporters of the no-fault legislation in 1989 and 1990, now opposed to no-fault.[51] The consumer group the Proposition 103 Enforcement Project argued that no-fault raised insurance rates. Project staff member David Link argued that seven of the ten states with the highest insurance rates also had no-fault laws (Shinkman, 1995).

---

[50] Other "pay-at-the-pump" plans were considered in Colorado, Massachusetts, Nevada, Texas, Florida, Louisiana, and Hawaii (Insurance Information Institute, 2007).

[51] Harvey Rosenfield's former organization, Voter Revolt, which had been opposed to no-fault in the 1989 cycle of voter initiatives, had, by 1996, changed its position and decided to support no-fault.

CTLA, now Consumer Attorneys of California, mounted a media campaign to oppose the proposition and, in a reversal of the 1988 ballot-initiative experience, far outspent its opponents and argued that no-fault was unfair to safe drivers. One television advertisement argued, "His bad driving injures you. No-fault says that the fault is yours, rather than his" (Schwartz, 2000, p. 643). Insurers, chastened by their earlier experience, played little role in the battle (Burke, 2002, pp. 131–132). The proposal was roundly defeated, with only 35 percent of voters supporting the measure (Sugarman, 1998, p. 310, n. 22).

The California experience with no-fault illustrated the political debate over no-fault in the nation. Broad evaluations of policy advantages and disadvantages were trumped by cost. The many other advantages of no-fault cited by O'Connell and his predecessors—broader coverage, more proportionality, faster payments, and fewer arbitrary factual determinations—were rarely mentioned in the debate (Burke, 2002, pp. 134–135).

The only argument not related to cost that was apparently important was that of personal responsibility: Voters were hostile to a shift away from individual responsibility for automobile accidents. As Burke (2002, p. 135) explained, "voters bristled at the thought that, as one of the anti-104 commercials put it, under no-fault, 'a bad driver is no longer responsible.'" The notion that auto accidents were as much a fault of systems as individuals also gained no traction. Instead, the idea that automobile accidents were the fault of bad drivers (inevitably not themselves) resonated.

## The Attempt to Enact Federal Choice No-Fault: 1998–2003

At the federal level, no-fault also proved unsuccessful. After unsuccessful efforts to enact a federal no-fault law in the late 1970s, no-fault proponents hoped that a new approach, one that allowed each consumer to choose to adopt or reject a no-fault plan, would be more successful.

In 1999, bipartisan legislation that would establish a choice auto-insurance plan in all states was introduced in both the U.S. Senate (S. 837) and the U.S. House of Representatives (H.R. 1475). Under this proposal, drivers would have been given a choice between a modi-fied version of their state's current insurance system (MCS) and an absolute no-fault (ANF) plan.[52] Under both bills, each state would have the right to reject the choice plan and retain its current auto-insurance plan.

RAND researchers projected that the proposal would have allowed drivers willing to waive their tort rights to buy personal-injury coverage for 54 percent less than coverage under their state's current system. This translated into a 22-percent savings on total auto-insurance premiums. Under the study's assumptions, the proposal would also have allowed drivers who preferred to remain in a system similar to the current one to do so, at essentially the same costs (Carroll and Abrahamse, 1998).

Advocates of the choice approach hoped that, by permitting indi-vidual drivers to choose whether to accept the no-fault plan's restric-tions on tort suits in exchange for reduced rates, opponent's arguments would be blunted. If a driver did not like no-fault, he or she did not have to adopt it. As Michael Dukakis (in the foreword of Lascher and Powers, 2001) put it,

> [T]hose of us who were pushing no-fault constantly found our-selves facing the argument from our opponents that by advocat-ing no-fault laws, we were depriving people of their right to sue the other guy who might have been at fault. Given the waste and unfairness that is inherent in the liability lottery that passes for

---

[52] Each state's current rules would govern the compensation of accident victims covered by MCS if they were injured by an uninsured driver or by a driver who elected MCS. Acci-dent victims covered by MCS who were injured by a driver who elected ANF could recover for both economic (medical bills, lost wages because of time off work, and other monetary losses) and noneconomic (e.g., pain and suffering) losses, to the degree that that driver was responsible for the accident. Any current state laws that applied to an accident victim's recov-ery (e.g., the tort threshold in a currently no-fault state) would apply as in the state's current system. However, under a new type of insurance coverage, *tort maintenance*, a victim's own insurer—not the ANF driver's insurer—would pay compensation to that victim. Accident victims covered by ANF would be compensated, by their own insurer, for their economic losses, up to the policy limit. They would neither recover from nor be liable to others for noneconomic losses. Any accident victim, regardless of insurance status, could seek compen-sation from a driver who injured him or her for any economic loss not otherwise covered by some form of auto insurance, to the degree that that driver was at fault for the accident.

an auto insurance system, I never bought that argument. But our adversaries did have a point. There was no question that under certain circumstances we were denying people the right to sue a potential wrongdoer and limiting their ability to collect damages for pain and suffering. Auto Choice eliminates that objection. (pp. ix–x)

Nonetheless, the bill attracted substantial opposition. Economist and Yale Law School professor George Priest (1998) criticized the bill for permitting high-risk drivers "to escape the consequences for the accident costs they impose on the more careful." This argument echoed the hostility to liability without fault that Jeremiah Smith (1914) made more than 80 years prior. Priest also argued that accident rates would go up as a result of dangerous drivers remaining on the roads. J. Robert Hunter (1997), director of insurance for the Consumer Federation of America (CFA), criticized the bill for being confusing. Ralph Nader, echoing the critics of workers' compensation, defended the idea of fault. He argued that "no-fault systems contradict the fundamental principle of American Justice that wrongdoers are held responsible for the harm they cause. By eliminating fault, no-fault, effectively treats good drivers and bad drivers the same" (Nader, 1999).

Others criticized the federal government's involvement in what had traditionally been a state matter. Defense Research Institute staff member Gerard T. Noce argued,

It is pretty clear that state laws respecting recovery for injuries in automobile accidents are not an appropriate subject for federal preemption. There is simply no national interest in mandating, or even in suggesting, a preferred method of resolving motor vehicle lawsuits. (Noce, 1999)[53]

While federal no-fault legislation was introduced for several years in the late 1990s, it never passed.

---

[53] See also Handley (1999), who argued that the American Bar Association opposes the legislation because there is "no justification for Congress to take action to fundamentally change the present laws in all the states."

## The Political Situation Today

After years of active support and advocacy, insurers and some consumer groups have cooled on no-fault, for different reasons. Despite this change, the overall situation in most states is stable.

Despite many years of active support for no-fault, State Farm and the other industry supporters of no-fault recently decided that supporting no-fault was simply not worth their efforts. According to Jeffrey O'Connell (2008), the industry supporters of no-fault found that, whenever they advocated for it, trial lawyers were able to successfully tap into a deeply rooted suspicion of insurance-company motives and able to counterpropose more regulation and investigation of purportedly outrageous insurance-company cartel profits. The industry eventually felt that it was consistently losing this political battle.[54]

Insurers also found that it was easier to directly attack policy proposals and initiatives that were inimical to their interests rather than try to propose a no-fault (or other) alternative. One insurer explained, "it is easier to run a 'no' campaign" to an adverse proposal than to propose a no-fault alternative.

Consumer groups are similarly lukewarm in their support of no-fault. Robert Hunter explained that CFA continues to support a true Michigan-style no-fault plan with a strict verbal threshold and large first-party benefits. But the fact that price reductions hoped for with other no-fault plans never occurred damped their enthusiasm (Hunter, 2008). CFA is far more enthusiastic about Proposition 103–style reform—increased direct regulation of insurers.

In the academy, no-fault also lost support. Schwartz (2000) attacked one justification of no-fault by arguing that automobile-accident cases were, in fact, *easier* to resolve than other tort claims, because traffic law was so comprehensive. The purported difficulty and expense of determining fault was a justification for no-fault. More generally, tort theorists emphasized the corrective-justice function of tort law over the need to generally compensate victims or spread losses

---

[54] Some insurers continue to support it. In 2007, for example, GEICO supported the continuation of no-fault insurance in Florida (Liberto, 2007).

(Coleman, 1992; Goldberg, 2003). Fault was central to this under-standing of tort law.

The argument for no-fault may have been weakened by the broad-ening of coverage in the tort system. For example, the replacement of contributory negligence with comparative negligence in every state in the past 30 years reduced the number of uncompensated victims (Kinzler, 2006, p. 14). States also eliminated other doctrines that pre-vented recovery, including host/guest doctrines, and reduced family, governmental, and charitable immunity. Similarly, the development and growth of UM and UIM coverage may also have reduced the risk that a victim in a tort state is uncompensated (Kinzler, 2006, p. 15).

No-fault was repealed in 2004 in Colorado, with the support of some of the insurance industry. Interestingly, the most-vocal propo-nents of no-fault were not insurers or consumer groups but rather the many medical providers (hospitals, doctors, ambulance services), for which it provided an excellent source of reimbursement of medical expenses. Average auto-insurance premiums dropped 35 percent from July 2003 to December 2007 (BBC Research and Consulting, 2008, p. 5). In contrast, the costs of inpatient medical care resulting from motor-vehicle accidents shifted from no-fault to Medicare, Medicaid, and the victims (BBC Research and Consulting, 2008, p. 10). Hospi-tals reported that reimbursement rates fell from 60 percent in 2002 to just 36 percent in 2006 after the repeal of no-fault. Emergency medical service (EMS) providers were affected in similar ways (BBC Research and Consulting, 2008, p. 12).[55]

In 2007, no-fault narrowly survived in Florida after an unusual three-month sunset period (Royse, 2007). While a few auto insurers supported no-fault, most supported its repeal (Zucco, 2006).

Despite the waning insurance and consumer-group support for no-fault, there are few signs that it will soon be repealed in most states where it presently exists. Similarly, there seems to be substantial con-sumer support for choice no-fault in at least some states. In Pennsylva-nia, a choice state, for example, slightly more than 50 percent of con-

---

[55] According to some insurers, many chiropractors who received a substantial portion of their income from no-fault have left the state.

sumers elect to forgo their right to recover in tort in exchange for lower rates. Despite the rejection of a federal no-fault choice plan, choice probably remains the form of no-fault that is most politically attractive.

## Conclusion

At its apogee in the late 1970s, no-fault appeared to many to be the best answer to long-chronicled problems with using the tort system to compensate victims of automobile accidents. Proponents of no-fault argued that it would eliminate the specter of uncompensated automobile-accident costs,[56] reduce the disproportionality between economic losses that victims suffer and the actual compensation provided by the tort system, and greatly reduce costs by eliminating recourse to the courts in all but the most serious cases. Most no-fault advocates thought that the reduction in costs would lead to reduced premiums, but this was only one of many criteria for evaluating the desirability of a system for compensation for automobile accidents.

In the past 30 years, however, the debate has shifted from the theoretical advantages of no-fault to what matters most to voters—premium cost (Davies, 1998, p. 847; Lascher, 1999). Once no-fault proponents could no longer credibly promise premium reductions, political support for no-fault cooled. The only argument not related to cost that appeared to resonate was that no-fault would unfairly exempt bad drivers from the consequences of their driving. The other arguments that no-fault proponents raised—reduced litigation and increased proportionality between compensation received and economic loss suffered—lost whatever political salience they had. As a result, policymaker, consumer advocacy–group, and insurer support for no-fault has waned.

---

[56] The passage of the Emergency Medical Treatment and Active Labor Act (Pub. L. 99-272, codified at 42 U.S.C. § 1395dd) requires emergency rooms to provide stabilizing treatment regardless of the ability to pay. As Schwartz (2000, p. 626) observed, this, in combination with the rise of public and private medical insurance, reduced the risk that a victim of a serious automobile accident would be wholly uncompensated and unable to obtain vital medical care.

The predominant influence of costs should come as no surprise. Human beings are particularly poor at estimating and thinking about the likelihood of improbable events—such as accidents (Svenson, 1981).[57] Individual voters, believing that they are safer than average drivers and will probably never be involved in an accident in which another is not at fault, focus on one thing: the premium they must pay. The other issues that proponents of no-fault raise—litigation costs, coverage for accidents with no at-fault driver, proportionality—therefore have relatively little political salience.[58]

But, if concern over consumer costs has come to dominate the debate, why have the costs been so high? Proponents of no-fault believed that, by reducing noneconomic damages and minimizing transaction costs, it would be possible to extend coverage *and* reduce costs. What went wrong? We now turn to the question of why the costs of no-fault have remained higher than expected.

---

[57] See also Kunreuther (1982). People tend to underestimate the likelihood of a low-probability event until one occurs. At that point, they overestimate the likelihood of a similar event's recurrence. See Mashaw and Harfst (1990), discussing the regulation of school buses in the wake of highly publicized school-bus accidents.

[58] See Liebman and Zeckhauser (2008), who argue that human cognitive frailties justify intervention in health-insurance markets.

# CHAPTER FOUR

# The Cost of No-Fault

Many no-fault proponents claimed that no-fault would reduce claim costs. These proponents argued that no-fault would reduce litigation, limit third-party claims (particularly for noneconomic damages), and simplify the process of determining who was at fault, reducing administrative costs enough to offset the cost of the more-generous first-party benefits available under no-fault. However, a number of researchers have argued that no-fault has actually *increased* insurance costs (Johnson, Flanigan, and Winkler, 1992; Rosenfield, 1998; Cole et al., 2008). And, as was discussed in the last chapter, the continuing high cost of no-fault was used as a key argument against it in California, Colorado, and elsewhere.

Is a no-fault regime a more or less expensive means of compensating victims for automobile-accident costs? And have those costs changed over time? In this chapter, we look at the available data and compare the auto-insurance premiums and costs of compensating victims of automobile accidents in states under no-fault, tort, and add-on systems from the 1980s to 2004. We conclude that auto-insurance premiums and expenditures for compensation are higher under no-fault, at least as it is currently used in the United States. In the next chapter, we address possible reasons for that finding.

The insurance premiums paid by consumers reflect numerous components, including costs of reimbursing individuals for injuries, property-damage reimbursements, administrative costs associated with claim management and company operations, investment income, taxes, and economic profits for insurers. Recent estimates by the Insurance

Information Institute (2009) indicate that 30 percent of earned premiums are spent compensating injury victims, with an additional 40 percent utilized for property-damage reimbursements and the remainder representing operating expenses and profits. Thus, injury compensation costs comprise a major component of the total cost of auto insurance.

From the consumer's perspective, a typical consumer policy is divided into a three major components: a written liability premium, which covers costs associated with compensating injuries; a collision premium, which covers property-damage costs; and a comprehensive premium that covers losses due to theft or other circumstances. In our analysis, we focus on the written liability premium, which we view as the cost component most likely to be affected by the insurance system. Written liability premiums represent the largest portion of the overall premium paid by consumers and heavily influence the total premium.[1] In some cases, we also examine injury compensation costs, because these data cover a wider range of years and allow us to examine the costs of specific coverage, such as BI and PIP. Unsurprisingly, average written liability premiums closely track per-vehicle injury compensation costs.

We first examine aggregate trends in liability premiums and injury compensation costs over time, focusing on states that maintained a single system over the entire period between 1980 and 2006. Our cost data for this analysis are drawn from the IRC *Trends in Auto Injury Claims* (2008) database. The data in these files are primarily derived from the Fast Track Monitoring System, which reports aggregate policy and cost data based on reports from participating insurers. Currently, insurers representing roughly 70 percent of the auto market are included in Fast Track. The cost data presented in this chapter represent costs of compensating claimants and do not reflect the administrative costs of managing claims.[2]

---

[1]   Looking across states between 2002 and 2004, the correlation between the average written liability premium and the total premium is 0.95.

[2]   The *pure premium*, one commonly used cost concept, includes both loss costs (payments made to victims) and loss-adjustment costs (costs of investigating and settling claims), and thus differs slightly from our cost measure.

By comparing cost trends in no-fault and add-on states, we can isolate the effects of limitations on lawsuits from the effects of PIP insurance coverage. As explained in Chapter Two, a no-fault regime typically consists of two related but conceptually independent policies: required first-party PIP insurance and a limitation on lawsuits against third parties. A conventional no-fault regime has both of these elements. Some states (add-on states) require or make available first-party insurance without any limitation on tort suits. Looking at cost trends in these states helps to separate the effect of PIP insurance from the effect of the limitations on third-party lawsuits. If first-party PIP insurance is the cause of cost differences, other factors being equal, we would expect costs in add-on states to track those of no-fault states. If cost increases are the effect of limitations on lawsuits, no-fault states should exhibit higher costs than add-on states.

Our analyses omit the choice systems operated by New Jersey, Pennsylvania, and Kentucky.[3] Because these states have fairly idiosyncratic systems and drivers may sort across coverages based on insurer marketing or unobserved preferences, we do not consider them as a separate group.

## Aggregate Cost Trends Among States

Figure 4.1 plots average written liability premiums for four insurance regimes: no-fault, pure tort, tort with mandatory PIP add-on coverage (mandatory add-on), and tort with optional PIP add-on coverage (optional add-on).[4] Several patterns in the figure are notable. Premiums

---

[3]  Although Kentucky ostensibly allows consumers to opt out of the no-fault system, policy defaults favor no-fault, and only a small fraction of motorists actually decline no-fault coverage, so this state is a de facto no-fault state. New Jersey's choice system has been repeatedly modified since the 1990s in response to high premiums, large numbers of uninsured motorists, and a partial unraveling of the insurance market in 1998–2002. Anecdotally, Pennsylvania has the best-functioning choice system, and substantial numbers of drivers in this state are covered under both the no-fault and tort regimes.

[4]  See Table 2.1 in Chapter Two for a listing of states in relevant categories. PIP policy data were not available for all states with add-on options. We exclude choice states and states that changed insurance regimes during the sample period from this analysis.

have been consistently higher in states offering PIP coverage, with the highest premiums occurring in no-fault states over the sample period. However, whereas the premium gap between no-fault and tort stood at $75 in 1987, this difference ballooned to almost $150 in 1993 before declining slightly in the late 1990s. More recently, the gap has widened, making premiums under no-fault 50 percent higher than those under tort by 2004. Costs also increased dramatically in the optional add-on states in the mid-1990s but recovered subsequently, reaching near parity with mandatory add-on states by 2000. Figure 4.1 indicates that liability premiums are higher in no-fault states and have become increasingly expensive in relative terms over time.

An obvious drawback to simple comparisons such as those in Figure 4.1 is that other state characteristics, such as the road system, demographic characteristics of the population, and regulatory structure, may affect the cost of auto insurance, and these factors may themselves be correlated with whether a state has no-fault. For example, suppose states with higher underlying accident costs were more likely to

**Figure 4.1**
**Trends in Average Written Liability Premium, by Insurance Regime**

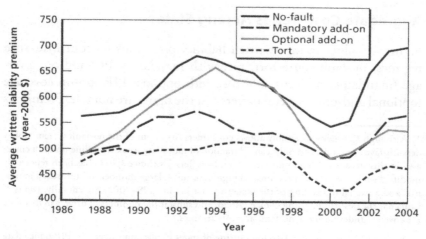

SOURCE: Authors' calculations from IRC (2008a, 2008b).
RAND MG860-4.1

adopt no-fault in an effort to control these costs. One could not fairly attribute subsequent high costs to the effect of no-fault.[5] Thus, some of the differences in Figure 4.1 may reflect factors other than the influence of the insurance system.

Factors affecting liability premiums across states include such characteristics as climate, road configuration, and vehicle usage patterns. These will impact injury loss costs because they affect the amount of injury-causing automobile activity within a state. In other words, some states are simply more likely to generate higher accident-insurance losses than others for reasons that have nothing to do with the kind of insurance regime they have. For example, we might expect higher accident costs in New Jersey than in Wyoming simply because New Jersey is more densely populated. Additionally, some premium differences likely represent general price-level differences across states—e.g., medical care may be more expensive in some states than others.

We can partially control for such interstate differences using property-damage costs, which should vary in tandem with many of these other factors. Following Cummins and Tennyson (1992), we divide injury costs (the major component affecting liability premiums) by average property-damage costs in a given state and year. By dividing injury costs by property damage, we can measure the effect of the liability rule apart from the underlying, state-specific factors that affect accident rate and costs.[6] Thus, property-damage costs can serve as a

---

[5]  This problem is known to researchers as *policy endogeneity*. Endogeneity makes it difficult to cleanly separate the effects of policies from the conditions that give rise to the policies. Here, the choice of liability regime is endogenous to the constellation of other factors that will also affect cost.

[6]  Because the liability rule (e.g., tort, no-fault, add-on) affects insurer costs associated with economic losses but not property damage, there is little reason to expect systematic differences in property-damage costs by insurance regime, except as reflected by the idiosyncratic differences in prices and injury-causing activity in the states included in each group. It is possible that the liability rule could have an indirect effect on property damage costs. See our earlier discussion of how no-fault reduced property-damage costs, presumably because some third-party property-damage claims were dependent on a claim for bodily injury. Alternatively, the liability rule could affect property-damage costs if it encourages unsafe driving, an issue to which we return below.

crude proxy to capture some of the interstate differences, other than insurance regime, that affect insurance losses.

Figure 4.2 plots the average injury loss per vehicle divided by the average property-damage loss per vehicle, by insurance regime. *Injury loss* is defined as the combined amount of loss per insured vehicle paid under BI, PIP, MedPay, UIM, and UM coverage.

Once we control for differences in the general price level and for the rate of auto accidents that result in property-damage claims, a slightly different pattern emerges. Between 1987 and 1995, no-fault, tort, and optional add-on states experienced similar injury-cost trajectories, with mandatory add-on states initially lagging but reaching parity by the mid-1990s. While relative costs continued to drop in optional add-on and tort states in the next ten years, they remained stable in no-fault and mandatory add-on states, leading these states to exhibit substantially higher relative costs by 2004. Thus, while no-fault and tort states were roughly comparable in the level of adjusted

**Figure 4.2**
**Ratio of Injury Loss to Property Loss per Insured Vehicle, by Insurance Regime**

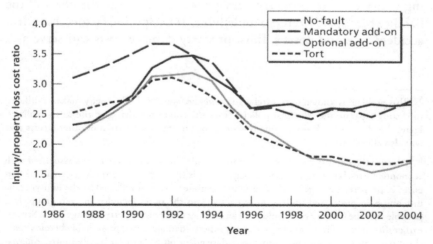

SOURCE: Authors' calculations from IRC (2008a, 2008b).
RAND *MG860-4.2*

injury costs in 1987, relative costs grew substantially in no-fault states by 2004.

Why did no-fault grow relatively more expensive? While a fuller analysis of the possible reasons for this cost difference awaits us in the next chapter, Figure 4.2 helps clarify the distinction between the effects of first-party medical benefits and the effects of limitations on lawsuits. The most intuitively plausible explanation of why no-fault is more expensive is that victims with first-party insurance (like the PIP required in no-fault and mandatory add-on systems) will use the medical system more than victims who must recover compensation from third-party insurers. The fact that adjusted injury costs were also high in mandatory PIP states supports this interpretation.

How might we interpret the cost trends in optional add-on states, which also offered PIP to at least some drivers but which saw lower adjusted costs, similar to tort states? One possibility is that, because individuals are not required to purchase PIP in optional–add-on states, insurers were able to effectively target PIP policies to individuals who were superior risks, allowing the insurers to better contain costs associated with first-party policies.

To understand the sources of some of the cost differences outlined in Figures 4.1 and 4.2, we now turn to one component affecting the average liability premium: BI claim–payment costs per insured vehicle. These costs primarily reflect compensation for third-party claims for bodily injury resulting from accidents. A key goal of no-fault was to reduce these costs by shifting compensation from the third-party BI liability system to the first-party PIP system by creating a threshold for access to BI compensation. Thus, we would expect BI costs to be substantially lower in no-fault states.

The data belie our expectations. Figure 4.3 plots BI costs per insured vehicle. Comparing no-fault to tort states, we see that, prior to the early 1990s, BI costs were indeed equal or lower in no-fault states but that, around 1993, this pattern reversed and that, since that time, BI costs have actually been *higher* in no-fault states. We address some possible causes of this surprising finding in the next chapter.

Prior to the early 1990s, the additional costs of PIP could be justified as providing somewhat lower BI costs (as was the intention of the

**Figure 4.3**
**Trends in Bodily Injury Paid Claim Costs, by Insurance Regime**

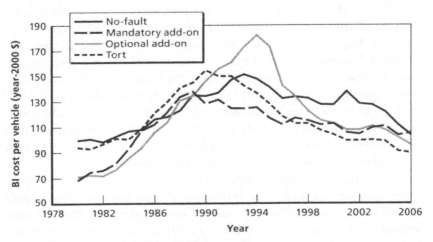

SOURCE: Authors' calculations from IRC (2008a, 2008b).
RAND *MG860-4.3*

original proponents of no-fault), but this rationale has disappeared, as BI costs have remained relatively high in no-fault states while dropping elsewhere. It is surprising to observe higher BI costs in no-fault states, given that victims are barred from filing BI claims unless their injuries exceed the relevant threshold.[7]

We now turn to tracing the paid claim costs of the first-party PIP coverages. Figure 4.4 plots trends in PIP costs exclusively. Since conventional tort states do not permit PIP coverage, there is no line for tort. Adjusting for the initial cost differences observed in 1980, a continuously running PIP policy under no-fault would have generated an

---

[7]  We also observe that both varieties of add-on states experienced BI costs that were similar to each other and to tort states in the early and later years of our sample but that there was a short-term spike in BI costs in optional add-on states in the 1990s. A comprehensive tort-reform package that was passed in Texas in 1995 likely contributed to the decline in BI costs in that state, although Maryland and Washington (two other optional–add-on states) both saw declines after peaks in the early 1990s as well.

**Figure 4.4**
**Trends in Personal-Injury Protection Paid Claim Costs, by Insurance Regime**

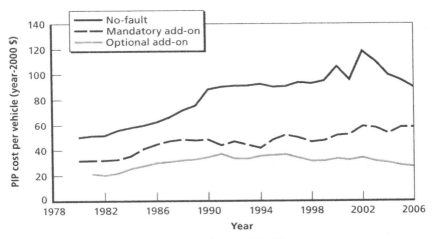

SOURCE: Authors' calculations from IRC (2008a, 2008b).
RAND MG860-4.4

additional $300 in costs between 1980 and 2006 beyond what a PIP policy would have generated in a mandatory add-on state.

Figure 4.5 shows that the first-party coverages generate higher costs in no-fault states than in optional– or mandatory–add-on states. One plausible explanation for this is the fact that PIP policy limits are higher in no-fault states, a factor that would increase costs, other things being equal. The limitation on lawsuits may also induce victims to bill more treatment to PIP policies than they would with the ability to recover from third parties. In optional–add-on states, PIP costs have remained relatively low. However, policy limits for PIP policies written in these states are modest relative to mandatory–add-on states, a feature that automatically limits costs.

The differences in the cost trajectories between BI and PIP are interesting in light of the fact that medical costs rose generally during the period in question. Relative to the general inflation rate, prices for medical care at the national level rose an additional 84 percent between 1980 and 2006.

**Figure 4.5**
**Trends in U.S. Medical Cost Inflation**

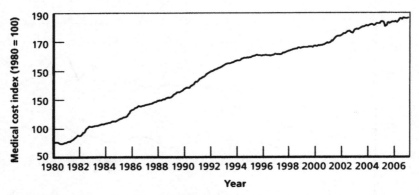

NOTE: This figure depicts trends in the "Medical Care" price component of the Consumer Price Index (CPI) for all urban consumers relative to "All Items." It thus measures the degree to which costs for medical care have outstripped general inflation between 1980 and 2006.
RAND MG860-4.5

Despite the fact that medical care comprises an important component of BI costs, average BI payments fell across states under all insurance regimes between 1994 and 2006. Growth in real average PIP claim payments was more in line with medical inflation, with payouts growing by 79 percent in no-fault states, 27 percent in optional–add-on states, and 84 percent in mandatory–add-on states between 1980 and 2006.

## Aggregate Cost Trends Among No-Fault States That Differ in Size and Threshold Type

Thus far, we have treated no-fault states monolithically, but, even within the group of no-fault states, there is considerable variation in the liability environment. Among no-fault states, three—Michigan, New York, and Florida—stand out as outliers, both because they are relatively populous states that include multiple large cities and because they operate under a verbal-threshold system. Most of the remaining no-fault states, such as Kansas, North Dakota, Utah, and Hawaii, have dollar thresholds and are much less densely populated.[8] It is therefore worth comparing these two groups of no-fault states.

Figure 4.6 plots BI plus PIP costs for Michigan, New York, and Florida (solid line) as compared to the smaller, dollar-threshold states. Absolute cost levels in the larger states are much higher than other no-fault states probably because they are more densely populated and more affluent. Interestingly, the verbal thresholds used by the larger states are thought to be more effective than monetary thresholds in reducing third-party claims, but whatever cost-reduction effect this might have had has been overwhelmed by other factors.

**Figure 4.6**
**Trends in Bodily Injury Plus Personal-Injury Protection Costs for No-Fault States**

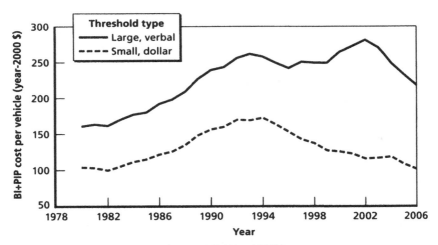

SOURCE: Authors' calculations from IRC (2008a, 2008b).
RAND MG860-4.6

---

[8]   Massachusetts represents somewhat of an intermediate case, in that it is fairly densely populated but also has a dollar-threshold system. Like the larger verbal-threshold states, injury cost levels in Massachusetts are relatively high, but the cost trends in Massachusetts are more similar to those of the other dollar-threshold states. Because it does not cleanly fit with either group of states, we omit Massachusetts from Figure 4.6.

Prior to 1994, the cost trends in the two sets of states are quite similar, with steady increases during the 1980s that then moderated. Since the mid-1990s, costs have fallen steadily in small no-fault states. In larger states, in contrast, costs rose until 2002 and have only begun to drop more recently. At a few points in the analysis that follows, we differentiate between the larger, verbal-threshold states and the other no-fault states, with an eye toward understanding factors that might explain the differences we observe in Figure 4.6. One message of Figure 4.6 is that cost containment may be more possible under some versions of no-fault, such as dollar-threshold systems implemented in smaller, less densely populated states.

## Aggregate Cost Trends in States That Repealed No-Fault

If no-fault does indeed affect insurance costs, then, in addition to observing cross-sectional cost differences between states under different systems, costs within states should also change as vehicles and drivers are moved out of no-fault coverages. That is exactly what we find. Over the period of available data, three states repealed no-fault statutes and reverted to a tort system: Georgia in 1991, Connecticut in 1994, and Colorado in 2003. Figure 4.7 plots trends in average written liability premiums in each of these states.

Figure 4.7 reveals a striking pattern of substantial cost decreases in all three states following the repeal of no-fault. Liability premiums in Georgia reached a steady state of approximately $360 following the no-fault repeal, a decline of 20 percent relative to costs immediately prior to the change. In Colorado, one year following the no-fault repeal, average premiums had dropped by more than $100 per insured vehicle. Connecticut experienced similar precipitous cost decreases following its return to tort. Given that all three states experienced periods of cost growth in the years immediately prior to no-fault reform, it is possible that some of the declines depicted in Figure 4.7 reflect mean reversion. However, it seems unlikely that these states would have experienced such large and abrupt cost reductions absent the change in insurance regime.

**Figure 4.7**
**Trends in Average Liability Premiums for Repeal States**

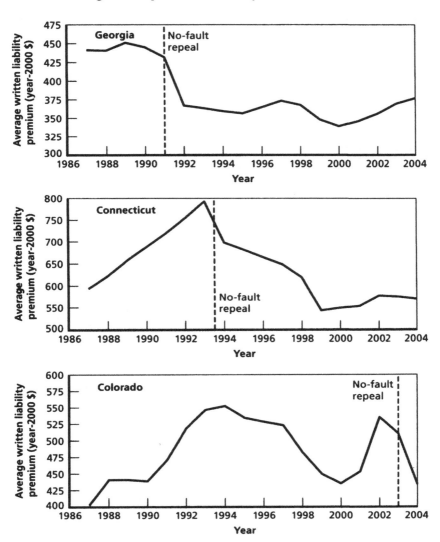

SOURCE: Authors' calculations from IRC (2008a, 2008b).

RAND *MG860-4.7*

## Conclusion

In summary, between the 1980s and 2006, both average liability premiums and premium growth were higher in no-fault states than other states, particularly tort states. These differences persist after adjusting for property-damage costs to account for variation in general inflation and accident prevalence across states. We also found that states that repealed no-fault laws saw substantial drops in liability premiums. Taken together, these facts indicate that no-fault has been a more expensive auto-insurance system. Mandatory–add-on states also exhibit higher costs than tort states, suggesting that widespread availability of PIP benefits plays a role in differential costs. In the next chapter, we examine possible explanations for the higher costs of no-fault relative to other systems.

# Why Have No-Fault Regimes Been More Expensive Than Anticipated?

As explained in Chapter Three, cost reduction was one of several arguments raised by proponents of no-fault automobile insurance. Over time, however, the political debate over no-fault focused on consumer cost. As we saw in Chapter Four, the perception that a no-fault regime was often more expensive than tort is confirmed by the data. In this chapter, we investigate possible reasons for this counterintuitive finding: Why would a system whose goal was to simplify the claim process and reduce costs end up being more expensive?

We begin with some simple math: The total cost of claims equals the number of claims multiplied by the average cost per claim. Higher costs in no-fault states may therefore represent either (1) a larger number of claims or (2) higher costs per claim.

We first consider whether no-fault is more expensive because there are more claims. No-fault states may produce more claims because there are more accidents or because it is more likely that an injured driver will file a claim when an accident occurs. We begin by examining the evidence for these effects. Our review of crash-data studies combined with observations of states repealing no-fault convinces us that higher accident frequency is not the culprit explaining the greater-than-expected costs of no-fault. We also examine direct measures of the probability of filing a claim after an accident and find little evidence of differences across systems.

The other alternative is that no-fault is more expensive because individual claims cost more. We will address a number of possibilities:

- Does no-fault provide higher reimbursement for a given injury? We examine survey data for evidence regarding the extent to which those under no-fault receive greater reimbursement.
- Does no-fault create greater incentives for fraudulent claiming? We analyze two types of fraud: (1) threshold overclaiming and (2) excessive claiming for injuries that are hard to verify.
- Are claimed work losses higher under no-fault?
- Does no-fault provide comparable compensation for noneconomic losses? If no-fault provides lower levels of reimbursement for noneconomic losses, this might counteract higher costs across other dimensions.
- Does no-fault encourage greater use of medical services?
- Is medical cost inflation higher in no-fault states?
- Is no-fault ineffective in barring claims from the third-party tort system? No-fault is predicated on the notion that the additional costs of providing more universal coverage can be offset by savings generated by removing cases from the legal system. An increase over time in the share of cases reaching trial or attorney involvement in no-fault states would likely contribute to increased costs.

Higher costs under no-fault may also simply reflect the fact that no-fault provides a higher-quality insurance product that is correspondingly more expensive. Although we are unable to directly relate quality differences to costs, we can examine whether no-fault is differentiated across some dimensions of quality. In particular, we examine the following:

- Does no-fault result in faster claim processing?
- Does no-fault create greater consumer satisfaction?
- Does no-fault reduce the need for litigation?

There are other possible explanations for the higher costs of no-fault that we were not able to examine. One possibility mentioned to us by insurers is that the necessity for each company to run two parallel claim-processing structures in no-fault states—one focusing on managing the medical costs associated with PIP claims and the other providing more-traditional processing of liability claims—contributes materially to the overhead associated with administering claims. Although proponents of no-fault saw cost gains to shifting claim administration from courts to insurance companies in the 1970s, given the huge rise in medical costs and the increasing complexities of managed care, such benefits, if they existed, may have diminished over time. Unfortunately, we lack data that allow us to reliably compare overhead costs across states over time. Throughout our discussion, we attempt to highlight such areas for which additional data collection might provide a richer understanding.

## Does No-Fault Lead to More Accidents?

If a no-fault regime leads to decreased driver safety and more auto accidents, then this factor would explain its rising costs. Basic economic models of liability, such as W. Landes and Posner (1987) and Shavell (1987), posit that individuals will adopt appropriate caution only when they bear the full costs of their actions. In these models, no-fault insurance, which removes liability for damages caused in certain classes of accidents, may induce drivers to drive more recklessly, secure in the knowledge that they will be made whole by their first-party insurance.

Although these models are both simple and somewhat intuitive, it is not clear that they describe real-world driving behavior. Fear of death or serious personal injury provides powerful incentives to avoid accidents no matter how generous the insurance. Moreover, the costs of causing an accident include both third-party and first-party personal injury and property damage as well as the costs of being cited, which may include future insurance-premium increases. Although no-fault limits first- and third-party personal-injury costs, it does so for only a subset of accidents and leaves other costs largely unchanged. Thus, the total effect of no-fault availability on the incentives for avoiding accidents may be relatively minor.

Recent theoretical work on the effects of no-fault that attempts to more realistically account for the actual characteristics of no-fault as practiced in the United States generates ambiguous predictions regarding the relationship between no-fault coverage and driver care. For example, Cummins, Phillips, and Weiss (2001) present a theoretical model that allows for experience rating and the possibility of errors in the assignment of negligence; in this model, the direction of the effect of no-fault on driver care depends on model assumptions, such as the degree of risk aversion and assignment-error rate. Liao and White (2002) model a mixed no-fault system, in which individuals have access to the tort system when losses exceed a particular threshold and demonstrate that the care levels may be above or below those under a pure tort system, depending on the level of the threshold.

Ultimately, whether no-fault leads to more-hazardous driving is an empirical question, and numerous scholarly studies have attempted to gauge this effect, if any. Table 5.1 summarizes eight previous studies of the effect of no-fault on fatal accidents.[1] A typical study compares fatal-accident rates across states covered by no-fault and other systems, controlling for aggregate driver and vehicle characteristics. As the table shows, half the studies claim that no-fault coverage increases fatal accidents, while the other half find no evidence of such an effect.

More-recent papers bring a greater level of methodological sophistication to the estimation of the effects of no-fault on fatal-accident rates. All employ panel data techniques, which identify effects of no-fault by comparing states that repealed no-fault to those that retained no-fault and thus control for macroeconomic trends and state-specific factors that do not vary over time. Using instrumental variables and selection corrections, Cummins, Phillips, and Weiss (2001) further attempt to account for the possibility that no-fault adoption may itself be related to accident rates. They find that accounting for potential endogeneity of no-fault substantially increases the estimated effects of no-fault on fatal accidents.[2] However, Derrig, Segui-Gomez, et al.

---

[1]    The listed studies focus on the no-fault experience in the United States; additional international studies include McEwin (1989) and Devlin (1992).

[2]    Even accepting the need to account for the endogeneity of no-fault laws, suitable instruments are difficult to isolate. The instruments used in existing studies, such as population density and party affiliation of legislators and the governor, may exert an independent impact on fatal accident rates. For example, population density is likely to affect traffic patterns, which affect accident rates, and Democratic lawmakers may be more willing to implement

**Table 5.1**
**Empirical Studies on No-Fault and Auto Fatalities**

| Study | Sample Period | Approach | Estimated Effect of No-Fault on Fatalities |
|---|---|---|---|
| Cohen and Dehejia (2004) | 1970–1998 | Panel analysis; differentiate effects of compulsory insurance and no-fault and instrument for adoption of no-fault | 6% increase |
| Derrig, Segui-Gomez, et al. (2002) | 1983–1996[a] | Panel analysis, seat-belt usage is primary explanatory variable of interest but includes no-fault status as a control and instruments for no-fault | No effect |
| Loughran (2001) | 1977–1989 | Difference-in-difference using both no-fault indicators and dollar thresholds | No effect |
| Cummins, Phillips, and Weiss (2001) | 1968–1994 | Two-step panel analysis designed to account for endogeneity of no-fault adoption | 13% increase |
| Sloan, Reilly, and Schenzler (1994) | 1982–1990 | Separate panel analyses by age, measure no-fault using the proportion of accidents with barred tort claims | 5% increase for adults |
| Zador and Lund (1986) | 1967–1980 | Panel analysis incorporating variations in dollar thresholds and claim adjudication | No effect |
| Kochanowski and Young (1985) | 1975–1977 | Repeated cross-section analysis | No effect |
| E. Landes (1982) | 1967–1976 | Panel analysis incorporating variations in dollar thresholds and claim adjudication | 2–15% increase |

NOTE: For all studies, the unit of observation is a state/year combination, and all studies include all states unless otherwise noted.

[a] All states are available for 1991–1996; four states are available for prior years.

other policies, such as gasoline taxes or graduated licensing requirements, that themselves affect the fatal accident rate. Such direct effects would invalidate the use of these factors as instrumental variables.

(2002) employ a similar approach and similar instruments and estimate a null relationship between insurance regime and motor-vehicle fatalities. Cohen and Dehejia (2004) present evidence that endogeneity of no-fault laws is not a major empirical concern but do find an association between no-fault and accidents after separately controlling for mandatory insurance. Loughran (2001) examines a broader set of outcomes, including a proxy for overall accident rates and rates of reckless driving, and finds little evidence that no-fault increases accidents. Thus, even among the more methodologically sophisticated recent papers, there is disagreement as to whether no-fault is associated with increases in fatal accidents. These results reflect the differences across studies in the empirical specifications and years examined. A persistent empirical challenge has been isolating the effects of what are likely small behavioral changes from the myriad of other factors that contribute to fatal accidents.

In a companion to this monograph, Heaton and Helland (2009b) provide new evidence regarding the effects of no-fault on driver safety. In contrast to previous studies that focus on fatal accidents, Heaton and Helland adopt an empirical approach that allows them to estimate the effect of no-fault coverage on both fatal and nonfatal accidents. Given that nonfatal accidents represent approximately 80 percent of all accident costs, understanding how the insurance system influences overall accident rates is important for evaluating the systems. They compare the frequency of accidents in which drivers were driving recklessly across drivers under no-fault and tort systems. Their approach allows them to control for prevalence and differences in vehicle characteristics, travel location, and driving conditions across driver types. Heaton and Helland are therefore able to obtain precise estimates suggesting that drivers under no-fault cause similar numbers of accidents and are involved in accidents of similar severity to those under tort.

In summary, although there are some theoretical reasons that no-fault coverage may raise costs by inducing less-careful driving, the empirical evidence is mixed. The study examining the broadest range of accident types (Heaton and Helland, 2009b) finds no evidence of an effect of no-fault on accident rates.

## Does No-Fault Lead to Higher Claiming Rates When Accidents Occur?

If it does not appear that there are more accidents in no-fault states, could it be that there are more claims filed per accident under no-fault? This seems an especially plausible hypothesis because one of the rationales of no-fault was that it would provide a source of compensation for all accidents and not just accidents in which someone else was at fault. In single-car accidents, for example, there is no other driver to sue, leaving the victim uncompensated from another driver's third-party auto insurance. No-fault insurance was supposed to make it easier to file claims. Rather than having to file against another driver's insurance company in a potentially adversarial posture, under no-fault, one could deal with one's own insurer. This is another theory as to why there might be more claims per accident under no-fault.

While plausible, the data does not support this explanation of the additional costs of no-fault. To address this issue, we analyzed detailed survey data from individuals who were involved in automobile accidents. In 1986, 1992, 1998, and 2002, nationally representative surveys of individuals injured in auto accidents were conducted on the IRC's behalf to obtain data about patterns in claiming, injuries, and costs.[3] Based on an initial screen, a sample of households that experienced a recent auto-related injury were identified and mailed questionnaires. Survey questions covered a variety of topics, including the nature of injuries sustained, sources of compensation, use of attorneys, and consumer-satisfaction measures.

Because the surveys include information about those in accidents regardless of whether they filed claims seeking reimbursement from their auto insurer, they permit us to account for the possibility that the systems themselves may affect an individual's willingness to purchase insurance or file a claim after experiencing an injury. To ensure

---

[3] These data are described in greater detail in several publications, including *Claimant Satisfaction in Auto Accident Cases* (All-Industry Research Advisory Council, 1989b) and *Paying for Auto Injuries: A Consumer Panel Survey of Auto Accident Victims* (IRC, 1994b, 1999b, 2004).

adequate samples for individual states, we pooled the data across years into two groups. We pool data from 1986 and 1992 and separately pool data from 1998 and 2002 in order to examine how quality changed during the 1990s. In order to ensure a comparable set of states across years, we also omit states that changed no-fault status and choice states from the analysis. Our total sample size is 7,968 respondents for the earlier group and 8,043 respondents for the later group.

As when drawing conclusions from any survey evidence, the problem of nonresponse bias exists. If the individuals most likely to return the IRC survey are systematically different from the larger universe of individuals involved in auto accidents, conclusions drawn from the survey evidence may not reflect the overall population. This is particularly true for mail surveys, which require respondents to fill out and mail a form. Since this process has some similarities to filing and prosecuting a claim, it is possible that the survey data may underrepresent individuals who do not file claims. Additionally, individuals may imperfectly recall the circumstances of their injuries or claims. Finally, they may be unaware of some aspects of claim handling, such as subrogation among insurers and whether, for example, the consumer's health insurer or auto insurer ultimately paid for medical costs. Thus, we interpret this data with some caution.

We also note that this and subsequent comparisons do not control for all factors that differ across states and may affect claiming behavior. Some of the differences in claiming behavior between no-fault, add-on, and tort states undoubtedly reflect differences in their population characteristics and legal and health-care environments as opposed to direct effects of the insurance system. At the same time, simple comparisons are likely to provide some insights into the cost differences documented in Chapter Four.

Table 5.2 reports the likelihood of filing a claim seeking reimbursement for losses of any kind from auto insurers after an accident. These averages have been regression-adjusted to account for any differences across systems in the overall amount of economic losses, which is

**Table 5.2**
**Percentage of Accidents with Filed Claims**

| Reporting Period | Tort | No-Fault | Add-On |
|---|---|---|---|
| 1986 and 1992 | 87.0 | 87.8 | 88.8* |
| 1998 and 2002 | 81.4 | 82.4 | 83.2 |

SOURCE: Authors' calculations from IRC consumer-survey data.
* = statistically significantly different from the value for tort states at the 5% level.

obviously an important determinant of claiming behavior.[4] Although claim-filing rates are slightly higher in no-fault and add-on states than in tort states, except for add-on states in the earlier period, these differences are not statistically significant. The small number of claims from mandatory–add-on states precludes analysis of those states as a separate group.

Claiming rates are similar across systems. This comparison of claiming rates provides direct evidence that the higher costs in no-fault do not simply reflect a willingness of consumers to file claims under no-fault that they would otherwise be unwilling to file under a tort system.[5] Thus, the additional costs of no-fault do not appear to reflect a higher rate of claiming per accident under no-fault.[6]

---

[4]   In particular, taking an individual as a unit of observation, for each time period, we estimated a regression of a 0-1 indicator for whether a claim was filed on indicators for residence in a no-fault state, residence in an add-on state (thus leaving tort residents as the omitted group), the log amount of reported economic loss, a missing indicator for the economic-loss variable, and year of survey fixed effects. This and all subsequent regressions were estimated using Stata version 9.2.

[5]   Also, it does not appear that the higher costs of no-fault can be attributed to inclusion of drivers who would otherwise be uninsured, since such differences should be apparent in claim rates. State-level UM rates estimated by the IRC (2006) are not correlated with no-fault status.

[6]   Interestingly, over time, the probability of filing a claim has dropped in all three systems.

## Are Costs per Claim Higher for No-Fault?

In the previous two sections, we considered and rejected the possibility that no-fault results in more claims either because it causes more accidents or because it causes more claims per accident. If we eliminate these explanations for no-fault's higher costs, then costs per claim must be higher in no-fault states. We now examine why this might be.

We first consider whether no-fault might reimburse more of a victim's costs more quickly than other systems. We consider whether no-fault reduced trial litigation. We then consider various measures of the incidence of fraud and overclaiming, and the extent to which regimes vary on these measures. Finally, we consider the factor to which many people we interviewed attributed no-fault's surprisingly high costs: no fault's failure to control medical costs as effectively as other regimes and a shift in medical costs from accident victims' first-party medical insurance (in tort states) to their first-party auto insurance (in no-fault states).

### Does No-Fault Provide a More Victim-Friendly but More Expensive System?

One view of the no-fault/tort distinction is to conceptualize the two systems as representing different products, with no-fault providing a more victim-friendly product at a higher cost and tort providing a less attractive product at a lower price. Thus, some of the higher costs of no-fault documented in Chapter Four may simply represent better coverage provided through this system. In this section, we first examine survey data for evidence regarding the extent to which those under no-fault receive higher reimbursement. We also examine other dimensions of quality, such as consumer satisfaction and payment speed, that may not directly contribute to claim costs but may generate administrative costs. To examine coverage quality over time, we use the same consumer survey sample just described.

## Does No-Fault Offer Higher Reimbursement to Victims Than Tort Does?

Our analysis shows that no-fault does, in fact, offer slightly higher reimbursement rates than other regimes. Table 5.3 shows the proportion of economic losses that were reimbursed by insurers or other sources in the different regimes.

This measure indicates the extent to which individuals report paying out of pocket for economic expenses incurred as a result of motor-vehicle accidents.[7] We code compensation at levels beyond reported economic losses (because of payments for general damages, for example) as representing full reimbursement. In all three systems, reimbursement rates have been fairly stable over time, and tort and add-on systems achieve similar levels of reimbursement. Consonant with the intent of no-fault designers, consumers in no-fault states report higher levels of reimbursement, with victims receiving an additional 5–8 percent of economic losses reimbursed. Relative to the median claim size of $3,000 in 2002, this difference represents an additional $150 in compensation per claim. Other things being equal, we expect this higher level of reimbursement to explain some of the extra costs of the no-fault system. At the same time, given that relative reimbursement rates have remained fairly stable over time, the higher

**Table 5.3**
**Percentage of Economic Losses Reimbursed**

| Reporting Period | Tort | No-Fault | Add-On |
|---|---|---|---|
| 1986 and 1992 | 80.4 | 87.9** | 79.8 |
| 1998 and 2002 | 79.7 | 85.7** | 79.0 |

SOURCE: Authors' calculations from IRC consumer-survey data.

** = statistically significantly different from the value for tort states at the 1% level.

---

[7] We emphasize that the survey data report consumers' responses about their economic costs, which likely do not reflect the total costs of treatment. For example, consumers are unlikely to have information about payments made to their health provider from auto or private health insurers, and the source and size of such payments may differ radically across insurance systems.

reimbursement provided to victims under no-fault seems a less plausible explanation for the change in no-fault's relative costs.

In addition to providing greater overall compensation, no-fault systems may affect the willingness of accident victims and medical providers to seek compensation from auto insurers as opposed to other potential providers of compensation, such as private health insurers or the workers' compensation system. This could raise the costs that auto insurers face under no-fault, even if actual economic losses are similar across the systems.

Table 5.4 shows that consumers report that the auto-insurer share of the total reimbursement is similar between no-fault and tort states and has risen only slightly over time.[8] Thus, the additional costs of no-fault do not appear to simply reflect cost shifting from other providers toward auto insurers.

## Does No-Fault Result in Faster Claim Processing?

One persistent complaint leveled by no-fault proponents against the tort system was that third-party liability insurance companies would be very slow to settle claims. Detractors argued that insurance companies would process claims slowly and put pressure on impoverished victims to settle for small amounts so that the victims could pay their medical

**Table 5.4**
**Percentage of Reimbursement Borne by Auto Insurers**

| Reporting Period | Tort | No-Fault | Add-On |
|---|---|---|---|
| 1986 and 1992 | 73.4 | 74.0 | 75.8 |
| 1998 and 2002 | 76.8 | 75.8 | 78.1 |

SOURCE: Authors' calculations from IRC consumer-survey data.

---

[8] Consumers may not report these data accurately. The consumer panel survey asks respondents to list their total "injury-related expenses to date, regardless of who paid them." They are then asked to estimate the amount paid to date by source; included among the possible sources is "Health Insurance/HMO [health maintenance organization]." It is possible that consumers do not accurately report the percentage of economic costs paid by a particular category of insurers because they are ignorant of exactly who pays which bills. This may be particularly true for medical expenses billed directly to other parties.

bills. No-fault proponents thought that first-party insurers would want to satisfy their customers and would therefore pay claims more quickly. In fact, we find that no-fault regimes process claims more quickly.

The first-party columns of Table 5.5 examine the timing of first-party payments—payments to injured parties from their own insurer.

The table shows the likelihood that first-party insurers settle the claim within three months of the accident. In tort states, the usual first-party coverages (MedPay, UM, and UIM coverage) are adjuncts to the primary third-party coverage. In no-fault and add-on states, the primary coverage (PIP) is first-party. As a result, the relevant comparison to understand routine claim-processing speed is comparing the first-party figures for no-fault insurance to the third-party figures for tort (see shading). This shows that a substantially higher percentage of claims are resolved within three months in no-fault states than in tort states in both periods. In the first period (1986–1992), 55 percent of no-fault first-party claims were resolved within three months, whereas only 25 percent of third-party tort claims were resolved.

Because the survey questions on settlement speed do not clearly distinguish injury and property damage, settlement of both types of claims are likely represented in these data, and we again control for the amounts of reported economic loss to allow for the possibility that more-complex claims require longer processing time.[9] For first-party claims, there is evidence of slightly faster claim processing in add-on states in the earlier period but similar processing times across the three systems more recently. Claim-processing times have generally slowed between the two periods, with an additional 15 percent of claims taking beyond three months to settle by 2002.

The third-party data in Table 5.5 show how quickly insurers process third-party claims, and a different pattern emerges. On average, third-party claims are roughly half as likely as first-party claims to

---

[9] In particular, as for Table 5.2, we estimated these proportions using a linear probability model in which we regressed an indicator for whether a claim was handled within three months on indicators for residence in a no-fault state, residence in an add-on state, the log amount of reported economic loss, a missing indicator for the economic-loss variable, and year-of-survey fixed effects. Regressions were separately estimated for 1987–1992 and 1998–2002.

**Table 5.5**
**Percentage of Claims Settled Within Three Months**

| Reporting Period | Tort | | No-Fault | | Add-On | |
|---|---|---|---|---|---|---|
| | 1st-Party | 3rd-Party | 1st-Party | 3rd-Party | 1st-Party | 3rd-Party |
| 1986 and 1992 | 57.3 | 25.0 | 55.0 | 28.5* | 62.8** | 27.2 |
| 1998 and 2002 | 44.7 | 20.3 | 43.9 | 25.7** | 43.1 | 18.6 |

SOURCE: Authors' calculations from IRC consumer-survey data.
* = statistically significantly different from the value for tort states at the 5% level.
** = statistically significantly different from the value for tort states at the 1% level.

settle within three months, and processing speed has also decreased over time for these claims. However, in both the earlier and later period, there is a higher likelihood of rapid settlement of *third-party* claims in no-fault states, and the processing slowdown was least pronounced in these states. The fact that no-fault actually encourages faster handling of third-party claims is surprising, given that no-fault shifts simpler claims from the third-party to the first-party system, leaving more-complex and presumably more–difficult-to-process claims for third-party insurers. However, if insurers use rapid claim payment to deter individuals from seeking a remedy for injuries in the court system, the faster payment for injuries in no-fault states may represent a rational response of insurers to potentially higher costs of litigating these more-complex cases. Whatever the underlying explanations, these patterns indicate that victims under no-fault enjoy more-rapid handling of their primary claims. Although our cost measures in Chapter Four do not separately measure administrative costs of no-fault, it seems possible that this comparatively speedy processing may generate additional costs.

### Does No-Fault Create Greater Consumer Satisfaction?
Consumer-survey respondents were asked to rate their satisfaction with the amount and speed of reimbursement for accident-related losses using a four-point Likert scale. Table 5.6 reports the proportion of

**Table 5.6**
**Percentage of Victims Satisfied with Amount and Speed of Reimbursement**

| Reporting Period | Tort | | No-Fault | | Add-On | |
|---|---|---|---|---|---|---|
| | Amount | Speed | Amount | Speed | Amount | Speed |
| 1986 and 1992 | 69.4 | — | 71.4 | — | 70.3 | — |
| 1998 and 2002 | 62.6 | 92.2 | 64.2 | 96.1** | 63.4 | 91.6 |

SOURCE: Authors' calculations from IRC consumer-survey data.

NOTE: Consumer surveys occur every five years, so there are no data for intervening years. Also, speed data were not collected in 1986 or 1992.

** = statistically significantly different from the value for tort states at the 1% level.

individuals reporting that they were "very" or "fairly" satisfied with their reimbursement. Despite the fact that reimbursement rates and speed of processing are superior in no-fault states, consumer satisfaction on these two dimensions is only slightly higher in no-fault states.

The speed data indicate that, although satisfaction with the speed of reimbursement is high in all three systems, it is roughly 4 percentage points higher in no-fault states.[10] Thus, on satisfaction measures, we find some evidence of higher-quality coverage in no-fault states, which is consistent with our findings regarding actual reimbursement rates and payment timing.

If no-fault establishes higher expectations for consumers, we might expect such similarities in ultimate satisfaction level. It is therefore difficult to know whether this is a genuine measure of consumer indifference between regimes or merely an artifact of higher consumer expectations associated with no-fault.

To sum up, one of the reasons that per-claim costs are higher under no-fault regimes is that no-fault is slightly superior to other regimes on the amount and speed of reimbursement. This superiority has not translated into substantially higher consumer-satisfaction ratings.

---

[10] Questions regarding satisfaction with reimbursement timing have been included in the survey only since 1997, so we are unable to look at comparable data for 1986 and 1992.

## Did No-Fault Reduce Litigation?

A key premise of no-fault was that it would reduce costs by reducing auto litigation. By diverting all but the most-serious cases from the third-party tort liability system to resolution between the victim and his or her insurer, proponents of no-fault believed that expensive and time-consuming auto-related litigation would be dramatically reduced.[11] How well has no-fault accomplished the central task of reducing litigation?

To assess whether no-fault reduces auto-related litigation, we first examine data from the Civil Justice Survey of State Courts. This survey collects data from a random sample of civil cases disposed by trial in a particular year; data are available for cases closed in 1991–1992, 1996, and 2001.[12] Given that states differ in their overall volume of litigation due to differences in population, laws, and legal institutions, we measure auto litigation using the proportion of overall civil trial cases that involved auto. This is a crude measure for a number of reasons, including the fact that it is influenced by factors not directly related to the auto-insurance system, such as settlement patterns for other types of cases and demographic and economic trends. Additionally, only a small proportion of total claims are actually taken to trial.[13] However, it has the advantage of providing a simple way of capturing the importance of auto-related disputes in the civil justice system. Other things being equal, if no-fault systems are successful in resolving auto-related injury claims without involving the legal system—a central goal of no-

---

[11] The costs of litigation are not fully borne by consumers and insurers and are not therefore fully reflected in our measures of claim costs. Litigation burdens the taxpayer-funded courts and may impose additional costs on individual drivers, who may find it more necessary to hire an attorney.

[12] Sample size is roughly 30,000 cases for 1991–1992, 9,000 cases in 1996, and 8,000 cases in 2001. Given that case data are typically stored at the local level, the survey utilizes a stratified sampling scheme, which involves randomly selecting counties for data collection. Thus, not all states are represented. In our analysis, the add-on states are Wisconsin, Texas, and Washington; the no-fault states are Florida, Massachusetts, Michigan, Minnesota, New York, and Hawaii, and the tort states are Arizona, California, Illinois, Indiana, Missouri, Ohio, and Virginia (BJS, 2004, 2005, 2006).

[13] In the 2002 BI closed-claim data, 12 percent of claims result in lawsuits and 1 percent of claims are taken to trial.

fault advocates—auto torts should comprise a smaller proportion of the trial caseload in no-fault states.

Figure 5.1 shows the proportion of civil cases involving auto, by year and insurance regime.

Over the entire period in question, an average of 29 percent of civil cases involved auto in no-fault states, versus 33 percent for both add-on states and tort states—differences that are statistically significant. For cases closed in 1992 and 1996, the auto share is similar across all three insurance regimes, but no-fault states experienced a decline in auto cases by 2001 that did not occur in other states.[14] Thus, auto accident–related trial litigation is less common in no-fault states.

Another way of measuring the amount of litigation is to see whether automobile-accident victims in tort or no-fault states are more or less likely to hire attorneys. The consumer panel surveys, described

**Figure 5.1**
**Trends in Auto-Related Trial Litigation**

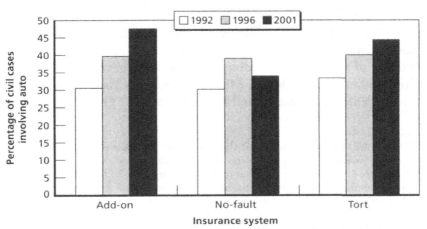

SOURCE: Authors' calculations from data from the Civil Justice Survey of State Courts.
RAND MG860-5.1

---

[14] Interestingly, in the closed-claim data, for BI claims, we see evidence that the proportion of claims that resulted in lawsuits fell between 1987 and 2002 across all insurance regimes.

previously, include questions about whether individuals hired an attorney that allow us to track attorney utilization across states over time. We find that, while victims in no-fault states were less likely to hire attorneys in the earlier 1986–1992 period, by the 1997–2002 period, the figures had become very similar.

Table 5.7 plots the proportion of respondents who hired an attorney in conjunction with their auto-related injury claim for the 1986–1992 period and the 1998–2002 period.[15]

Although the absolute changes are modest, there was a statistically significant increase in the use of lawyers in no-fault and add-on states during the 1990s. In tort states, in contrast, attorney involvement was stable. This suggests that the small advantage that no-fault possessed in the earlier period on this metric eroded over time.

The fact that use of attorneys for first-party claims was similar across the three systems and actually fell during this period suggests that growth in attorney use was caused by increases in third-party liability cases. Over time, no-fault became less effective in delivering on one of its original promises: minimizing the need for lawyer involvement in resolving claims.

This finding is also consistent with patterns on actual litigation volume observed in several states. Figure 5.2 plots the per capita number of new auto case filings in state trial courts for a group of three no-fault states (Florida, Michigan, and New York) and three tort states (California, Arizona, and North Carolina).[16] Data for the figure

[15] As in Tables 5.2 and 5.5, these results have been regression-adjusted to account for different levels of economic loss across residents of no-fault, add-on, and tort states. In particular, we estimated linear regression models at the individual level, in which we regressed an indicator for whether an individual hired an attorney on indicators for residence in a no-fault state, residence in an add-on state, the log amount of reported economic loss, a missing indicator for the economic-loss variable, and year-of-survey fixed effects. Regressions were separately estimated for 1987–1992 and 1998–2002. The sample for the analysis of attorney use for first-party claims is restricted to those who filed first-party claims. Regression results are available upon request from the authors.

[16] This set of states does not represent any selection on our part, but rather includes all of the no-fault and tort states that consistently reported auto case data to the National Center for State Courts. Examining the states individually reveals that, among the tort states, California and Arizona exhibited declining trends, while North Carolina exhibited a stable trend.

**Table 5.7**
**Percentage of Victims Hiring Attorneys**

| Reporting Period | Hired Attorney for Any Reason | | | Hired Attorney for Assistance with First-Party Claims | | |
|---|---|---|---|---|---|---|
| | Tort | No-Fault | Add-On | Tort | No-Fault | Add-On |
| 1986 and 1992 | 40.7 | 37.5** | 39.7 | 13.3 | 13.8 | 10.6 |
| 1998 and 2002 | 39.8 | 40.1 | 42.7* | 10.0 | 11.1 | 9.2 |

SOURCE: Authors' calculations from IRC consumer survey data.
* = statistically significantly different from the value for tort states at the 5% level.
** = statistically significantly different from the value for tort states at the 1% level.

**Figure 5.2**
**Trends in Litigation Volume in Selected No-Fault and Tort States**

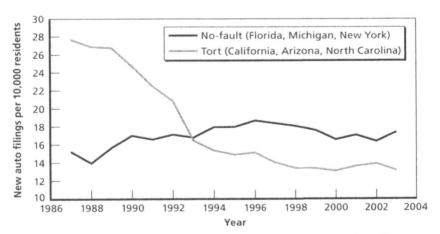

SOURCE: Authors' calculations from National Center for State Courts State Court Processing Statistics data.
RAND MG860-5.2

Among no-fault states, Florida had a stable trend, Michigan had a modestly declining trend, and New York had a rising trend.

are drawn from the *State Court Statistics* series (NACJD, 2005, 2006, 2007a, 2007b). In the three largest no-fault states, auto filings have been relatively stable over time, and litigation rates were substantially below those of the sampled tort states in the 1980s. However, during the 1990s, litigation rates fell substantially in the tort states, rendering tort and no-fault more comparable by the end of the data period.[17] Although the data in Figure 5.2 represent only a handful of states, they are consistent with the conclusion that no-fault's advantage at minimizing litigation has eroded over time.

How do we reconcile this evidence with that from Figure 5.1, which showed that auto trials were less likely in no-fault states? One interpretation of the combined evidence from Figures 5.1 and 5.2 is that there has been some relative increase in legal tort claims in no-fault states but that these additional claims have generally been settled prior to trial.

The fact that no-fault has become less effective at limiting litigation over time can be partly attributed to features of the thresholds used to determine which cases are eligible for tort recovery. In dollar-threshold states other than Hawaii, thresholds are set in nominal dollars and adjusted infrequently. General growth in the level of prices over time then causes an increasing share of cases to breach the dollar threshold. In verbal-threshold states, thresholds can weaken due to expansive judicial interpretations of the types of injuries that overcome a threshold. Litigation growth is a natural consequence of weakened no-fault thresholds.

To summarize up to this point, we have found evidence that no-fault systems provide reimbursement for a larger proportion of economic losses, greater satisfaction with the speed of payment, and faster resolution of third-party claims. Thus, part of the high cost of no-fault may reflect the higher quality of the insurance coverage provided under

---

[17] One reason for the decline in litigation in tort states is a fall in accident rates. Between 1988 and 2006, the average number of property-damage claims per hundred insured vehicles for California, Arizona, and North Carolina dropped from 3.99 to 3.53, a decline of 12 percent. However, it is notable that the property-damage claim rate in Florida, Michigan, and New York also dropped from 4.42 to 3.75 over the same period, even while there was little change in the litigation rate.

this regime. We have also shown that, while auto cases represent a smaller proportion of cases actually reaching trial in no-fault states, attorney involvement in cases has increased modestly over time in no-fault and add-on states relative to tort states, and total auto litigation volume has become more comparable between tort and no-fault states. Although our data on this point are not fully conclusive, they suggest one factor that may have contributed to the increase in costs associated with no-fault. We now address the extent to which the different regimes encouraged or discouraged fraudulent claiming.

### Does No-Fault Create Greater Incentives for Fraud?

In this section, we address the apparent role of fraud in increasing insurance costs under different insurance regimes. Originally, no-fault was thought to eliminate most incentives for fraud by eliminating noneconomic damages and by shifting compensation from the tort system to a first-party insurer.

Anecdotally, insurance-company representatives told us that first-party insurance fraud grew exponentially in the 1990s, as organized fraud rings discovered they could exploit no-fault as well as tort.[18] The growth of fraud in first-party insurance took the insurance industry by surprise: Originally, these claims were thought to be easier to manage than third-party claims and less likely to involve fraud, since general damages were not necessarily involved. According to some claim investigators with whom we spoke, large-scale organized fraud has played a large role in rate increases in the past ten years in no-fault states.

---

[18] A classic form of tort auto-insurance fraud is the "swoop-and-squat" planned accident. An old car slams on the brakes in front of a heavily insured commercial vehicle, hoping to provoke a rear-end collision. The occupants of the passenger vehicle then sue the owner of the commercial vehicle. Because the commercial vehicle rear-ended the passenger vehicle, it appears as though the commercial vehicle is at fault, leading the vehicle's third-party insurer to quickly settle with the (usually multiple) occupants of the passenger vehicle.

In no-fault states, according to insurance-fraud investigators, doctors were sometimes involved, providing a standard battery of numerous "treatments," including physical therapy, chiropractic therapy, acupuncture, at sham clinics. Insurers would be directly billed by the sham clinic for these "treatments." According to insurers, the risk of a first-party bad-faith claim for failure to promptly pay claims hindered adequate investigation into fraudulent claims, in New York especially.

Unfortunately, we cannot directly measure fraud. Instead, we identify claiming behavior that appears to be affected by the incentives of the insurance regime rather than the existence of an underlying injury. Consistent with the literature, we refer to such behaviors generically as *fraud indicators*, although the behaviors we describe may not, in all cases, meet the legal definition of fraud.

A substantial research literature is devoted to examining insurance fraud generally and the relationship between the auto-insurance regime and auto-insurance fraud specifically. Derrig (2002) provides a good overview of academic research on insurance fraud.[19] Existing research has identified a number of indicators for suspicious auto claims that vary according to the insurance system, including hard-to-verify injuries (Abrahamse and Carroll, 1995), claimed losses just above tort thresholds (Derrig, Weisberg, and Chen, 1994), and use of some alternative medical providers (IRC, 2007). Scholars have also examined how the potential for fraud and features of the tort system affect optimal claim-payment strategies for insurers (Crocker and Morgan, 1998; Crocker and Tennyson, 2002; Loughran, 2005). An additional strand of the research literature investigates statistical methods for detecting fraud, the sophistication of which has substantially increased in recent years (e.g., Artís, Ayuso, and Guillén, 2002; Viaene, Dedene, and Derrig, 2005).

Our analysis of fraud relies on fraud indicators similar to those identified in the existing literature. However, in contrast to existing studies, which typically focus on a single state or look across states at a single point in time, our use of data spanning multiple states and years allows us to examine how suspicious claiming behavior has changed across systems over time.

We emphasize from the outset of our discussion that our available data provide us with an informative yet ultimately limited set of fraud indicators. Because of data constraints, we are unable to identify or analyze certain types of fraud that anecdotally appear to represent important cost drivers. For example, many experts attribute much of

---

[19] The accompanying articles in this volume of the *Journal of Risk and Insurance* provide additional detail on statistical methods to detect fraud.

the large decline in PIP costs in New York since 2002 to the disruption of organized fraud rings operating in New York City. However, we lack data sources that would permit a systematic examination of such organized fraud.[20]

### Threshold Overclaiming

Under all insurance systems, there is some incentive for claimants to generally exaggerate the cost of claims, either by submitting claims for nonexistent injuries or treatment or by inflating the reported cost of treatments actually received. No-fault and tort systems may differ in the types of incentives for overclaiming, however. A key difference between the systems is the limitation on noneconomic damages under no-fault. Noneconomic damages, typically for pain and suffering, often make up a sizable proportion of the overall damage award. Insurers sometimes calculate these noneconomic damages as a multiple of actual economic damages suffered by the victim. Because of this multiplier effect, victims have strong incentive to exaggerate the amount of economic losses claimed (absent a limitation on general damages), because each additional dollar of economic loss can potentially yield several additional dollars of payment.[21] In no-fault states or another regime that restricts noneconomic damages, claims falling below the threshold are subject to reimbursement for the amount of economic damages only, so there is less incentive to exaggerate these claims.

However, the existence of thresholds in no-fault states provides a different impetus for overclaiming that is not present in tort states. In

---

[20] A substantial challenge in providing a systematic study of auto-insurance fraud is the dearth of reliable data that track fraud complaints or prosecutions across localities over time. Some state fraud bureaus report aggregate statistics on an annual basis, but the quality and types of information reported vary substantially across jurisdictions. We also do not focus attention on types of fraud that are not directly affected by the liability system, such as staged auto theft.

[21] However, Galanter (1996) summarizes numerous studies suggesting that multipliers are higher for individuals with smaller losses than for those with large losses. Insurers may attempt to counteract victims' incentives to inflate claims by recognizing only a portion of claimed economic losses or adjusting downward damage multipliers for suspicious claims. Loughran (2005) and Crocker and Tennyson (2002) provide evidence of such behavior by auto insurers.

dollar-threshold states, there are particularly strong incentives to exaggerate claims near the threshold value, since such exaggeration allows the claimant to obtain noneconomic damages for not only the marginal dollars expended but also all the previous losses incurred.[22] There is also incentive to exaggerate to breach the threshold under a verbal threshold, but, depending on the state, such exaggeration may be difficult because verbal thresholds are typically tied to criteria, such as permanent disability, that are more easily verified.

To examine threshold overclaiming as well as other types of fraud, we turn to the IRC closed-claim databases. Every five years, IRC collects data from participating insurers on individual claims closed under BI, PIP, MedPay, UIM, and UM coverages during a two-week period. The claim data are tabulated from the records of individual insurers using a uniform coding scheme. Although participation is voluntary, typically insurers representing the majority of covered vehicles in the United States have elected to submit data, making the database broadly indicative of claiming patterns in the United States, with some state-to-state variation in covered market share. These IRC closed-claim data have been widely utilized in academic research on auto insurance.[23] We focus on the BI, PIP, and MedPay databases published in 1987, 1992, 1997, 2002, and 2007 (All-Industry Research Advisory Council, 1989a, 1989b; IRC, 1994a, 1999a, 2003, 2008b), which allows us to

---

[22] As a concrete example, consider a state with a monetary threshold of $3,000. Suppose that an accident occurs in a regime in which general damages are roughly double economic damages. A victim claiming $2,900 in economic losses would fall below the threshold and qualify for only $2,900 in compensation. However, a claim of $3,000 would breach the threshold and provide general damages, generating compensation of ($3,000 [economic damages]) + ($3,000 × 2 [general damages]) = $9,000. Thus, the marginal benefit of inflating the claim by $100 in this case is $6,100 ($9,000 − $2,900), a sizable incentive for exaggeration.

[23] More documentation regarding these data sets, including copies of some of the original survey instruments, are available in several publications, including *Compensation for Automobile Injuries in the United States* (All-Industry Research Advisory Council, 1989a), *Auto Injuries: Claiming Behavior and Its Impact on Insurance Costs* (IRC, 1994a), *Injuries in Auto Accidents: An Analysis of Auto Insurance Claims* (IRC, 1999a), and *Auto Injury Insurance Claims: Countrywide Patterns in Treatment, Cost, and Compensation* (IRC, 2003, 2008b).

observe between 40,000 and 80,000 claims each year.[24] The databases include a wealth of information regarding each claim, including policy coverages, claimants' demographic characteristics, accident and vehicle information, claimed injuries, medical utilization, lost wages, attorney use, and features of settlement.[25]

A simple method for detecting threshold overclaiming is to examine the distribution of claimed medical dollar loss amounts around the threshold value.[26] Without claim manipulation, we expect to observe roughly equal number of claims just above and just below the threshold. In the presence of overclaiming, there will be few claims just below the threshold and a large number of claims just above the threshold, which will generate an uneven distribution. Although intuitive, a drawback of this approach is that it is fairly data-intensive—adequately characterizing the entire distribution of claims requires a relatively large number of claims. Among the states with monetary thresholds, Massachusetts and Minnesota provide adequate numbers of observations (typically more than 500 observations per year) in the closed-claim data to allow us to identify threshold overclaiming if it occurs.

Figures 5.3–5.6 plot the cumulative distribution function (CDF) for loss amounts for four states. Loss amounts are measured in nominal dollars, and we separately depict the distributions in 1987, 1992,

---

[24] An additional database was published in 1977 by the All-Industry Research Advisory Council, but there are differences between this survey and subsequent surveys that make it difficult to draw comparisons across the surveys. For example, the 1977 survey does not clearly identify soft-tissue injuries and has only limited information on reported (as opposed to paid) medical losses. We thus do not utilize the 1977 survey for our analysis. Beginning in 1987, IRC maintained a more uniform set of questions and coding rules for these surveys, although there have been questions added and other minor changes across survey waves.

[25] The closed-claim data are not without drawbacks. Because they focus on filed claims, they fail to capture the experience of uninsured motorists; nor do they capture costs of auto injuries borne by other actors, such as individual victims, private medical insurers, or the workers' compensation system. Additionally, because of the sampling scheme, there are relatively few very large claims and litigated claims included in the database, yet these claims may be of particular interest.

[26] Following this approach, Carroll, Abrahamse, and Vaiana (1995) compare claim distributions for Hawaii and New York, and Derrig, Weisberg, and Chen (1994) do so for Massachusetts.

**Figure 5.3**
**Cumulative Distribution of Claimed Medical Losses in Illinois**

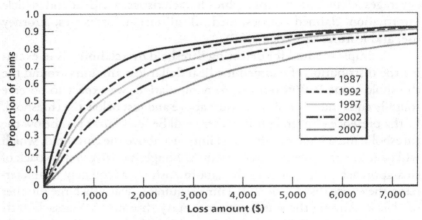

SOURCE: Authors' calculations from IRC closed-claim data (All-Industry Research
Advisory Council, 1989b; IRC, 1993, 2003, 2008b).
RAND *MG860-5.3*

**Figure 5.4**
**Cumulative Distribution of Claimed Medical Losses in New York**

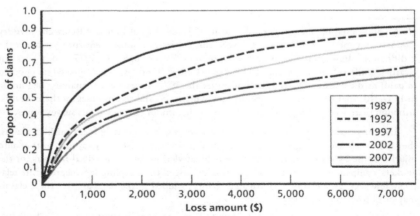

SOURCE: Authors' calculations from IRC closed-claim data (All-Industry Research
Advisory Council, 1989b; IRC, 1993, 2003, 2008b).
RAND *MG860-5.4*

**Figure 5.5**
**Cumulative Distribution of Claimed Medical Losses in Massachusetts**

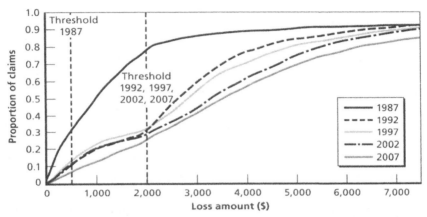

SOURCE: Authors' calculations from IRC closed-claim data (All-Industry Research
Advisory Council, 1989b; IRC, 1993, 2003, 2008b).
RAND MG860-5.5

**Figure 5.6**
**Cumulative Distribution of Claimed Medical Losses in Minnesota**

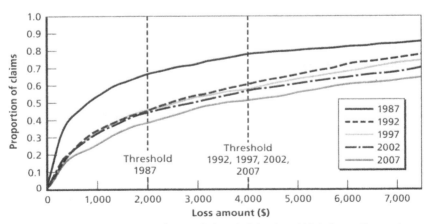

SOURCE: Authors' calculations from IRC closed-claim data (All-Industry Research
Advisory Council, 1989b; IRC, 1993, 2003, 2008b).
RAND MG860-5.6

1997, 2002, and 2007. The CDF represents the proportion of claims that fall at or below a particular dollar amount—for example, the fact that the distribution passes through the point 1,000, 62 in Illinois in 1987 indicates that 62 percent of all Illinois claims in this year involved medical losses of $1,000 or less. Figure 5.3 considers Illinois, a representative large tort state.[27] Because there is no tort threshold in Illinois, the Illinois distribution illustrates the appearance of a typical claim distribution. The fact that the distribution is moving to the right over time indicates that nominal average losses are growing over time, as one might expect. Figure 5.4 plots a similar set of distributions for New York, a verbal-threshold state. As in Illinois, the New York claim distributions are smooth, reflecting the fact that there are no particular incentives for overclaiming at specific dollar levels of injuries.

In the presence of claim manipulation to exceed dollar thresholds, cumulative distributions, such as those in Figure 5.5, will exhibit kinks because there will be fewer-than-normal claims slightly below the threshold. For Massachusetts, we observe clear evidence of such kinks in some years. In 1987, when the threshold was only $500, there is no obvious pattern of threshold overclaiming, but, at this point, the threshold was so low as to be easily breached with required medical treatment. Following the 1989 threshold increase, we see shifting of claims across the $2,000 threshold in 1992 and 1997. By 2002, there is still some evidence of shifting, although the erosion of the threshold due to medical cost inflation may have reduced threshold overclaiming, since a large proportion of claims could "naturally" fall above threshold. Shifting is not apparent in 2007.

Figure 5.6 plots the claim distribution for Minnesota, another state with a monetary threshold that increased during the 1990s. In contrast to Massachusetts, Minnesota does not show kinks at the threshold points, indicating that threshold overclaiming does not appear to be a problem in that state. It also appears that losses remained stable even in nominal terms in Minnesota through the 1990s.

---

[27] Plotting claim distributions for other large states, such as California or Ohio, generates similar insights.

Interviewees indicated that fraudulent claiming appears to be a greater problem in dense urban areas, which may explain why Massachusetts, with a substantial population in the Boston area, exhibits greater evidence of threshold overclaiming than Minnesota. However, the precise explanation for the differences between Minnesota and Massachusetts remains unclear.

In summary, consistently with the findings of past researchers, we are able to observe evidence of threshold overclaiming in some, but not all, dollar-threshold states.[28] We also see evidence from Massachusetts that this type of fraud increased over time as an unintended consequence of the increase in threshold. An important area for future research is identifying the factors that explain why some states with dollar thresholds experience higher rates of threshold overclaiming than others.

### Claiming for Hard-to-Verify Injuries

A number of studies have focused on soft-tissue claims as an indicator of overclaiming (Abrahamse and Carroll, 1995; Derrig, Weisberg, and Chen, 1994; Crocker and Tennyson, 2002). Soft-tissue injuries include sprains and strains of the neck, back, or other parts of the body. These injuries are typically more difficult to verify than other injury types because there are few available objective methods for their diagnosis. To examine how reporting of hard-to-verify injuries differs across systems and over time, we estimate regression models of the probability that a claim will involve soft-tissue injuries but not more–readily verified hard injuries. Our assumption is that hard injuries, such as fractures, serious lacerations, and burns, cannot be easily falsified and that claims involving these types of injuries are therefore legitimate. Clearly, some proportion of soft-tissue claims are also legitimate, but, other things being equal, we expect overclaiming to be higher in states in which a large proportion of claims involve hard-to-verify injuries.

---

[28] We also examined claim patterns in Utah and Kentucky, two states with dollar thresholds and a moderate number of claims in our sample. We see little evidence of threshold overclaiming in Utah and some evidence for Kentucky.

Figure 5.7 plots the regression-adjusted proportion of claims with hard-to-verify injuries, by insurance system over time. Our regression analysis controls for the time, location (urban/rural), vehicle count, impact severity, and reported injury severity of the accident, as well as age, gender, marital status, seat-belt use, and seat position of the victim. The chart thus reports the expected proportion of hard-to-verify claims, holding driver and accident characteristics constant at the levels observed in tort states.[29] Standard errors for these estimates mostly lie between 0.5 to 1 percent, so the differences across systems are generally statistically significant.

Several patterns are apparent upon examining Figure 5.7. For the entire period, hard-to-verify injuries were always less prevalent in no-fault states than in tort states, with the lowest prevalence in states with verbal thresholds. This pattern is consistent with an environment in which limited access to general (noneconomic—e.g., pain and suffering) damages under no-fault reduces incentives to engage in excess claiming. Across all systems, it is also apparent that there has been an increase over time in the proportion of claims involving hard-to-verify injuries. Whereas 62 percent of claims closed in 1987 involved such injuries, by 2002, this fraction was 72 percent.

Perhaps the most striking pattern in Figure 5.7, however, is the convergence between systems that occurred during the 20-year period between 1987 and 2007. If many claims involving hard-to-verify inju-

---

[29] In particular, we estimated claim-level probit regressions in which the outcome variable was a 0-1 indicator for a claim involving soft-tissue injuries and no hard injuries. Soft-tissue injuries were defined as strains or sprains of the neck, back, or other parts of the body, and hard injuries were defined as a fracture, concussion, brain injury, loss of body part, paralysis, or serious burn or laceration. The primary explanatory variables were indicators for whether a claim was subject to no-fault, optional add-on, or mandatory add-on provisions, with tort as the excluded category. Additional control variables included fixed effects for the hour, number of vehicles, and location type (five categories) of the accident; impact severity (six categories); injury severity (six categories); claimant age (five-year intervals), sex, marital status, seat position, and seat-belt use; and coverage limits of the insured (eight categories). Choice states and states that changed insurance systems between 1987 and 2007 were excluded from the sample. The regressions were separately estimated for each survey year. The figure was constructed by adding the average share of claims with hard-to-verify injuries in tort states to the appropriately transformed probit regression coefficient estimates for each insurance type. Results of these regressions are available upon request from the authors.

**Figure 5.7**
**Share of Claims with Hard-to-Verify Injuries, by Insurance Regime**

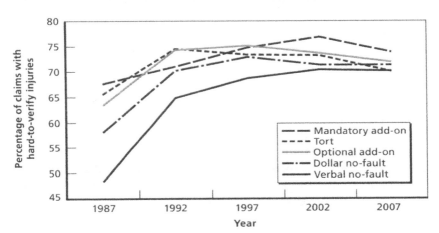

SOURCE: Authors' calculations from IRC closed-claim data (All-Industry Research
Advisory Council, 1989b; IRC, 1993, 2003, 2008b).

RAND MG860-5.7

ries do, in fact, represent fraudulent overclaiming, then the fact that
20 percent fewer claims in verbal-threshold states and 10 percent fewer
claims in dollar-threshold states involved such injuries indicates that
this type of fraud was much less prevalent in no-fault states, at least in
1987. However, by 2007, hard-to-verify injury claim rates were statistically indistinguishable across tort, dollar, and verbal no-fault states.
The increase in hard-to-verify claims in no-fault states during the
1990s coincides with a period in which auto-related litigation appears
to have declined less in no-fault states than in tort states. As relatively
more no-fault victims pursued tort litigation, the pattern of claiming
hard-to-verify injuries came to more closely resemble that in tort states.

Some critics of no-fault have argued that PIP is potentially particularly harmful with respect to overclaiming fraud because it can be
used to run up medical bills in order to (1) exceed tort thresholds and
(2) increase the likely size of general damages, which are thought to
have some relationship with medical damages. However, if the existence of PIP is a driving factor behind claims for nonexistent injuries,
we would expect to see particularly high incidence of hard-to-verify

injuries in mandatory add-on states, because these states combine universal PIP coverage with the broadest access to general damages. However, we do not see substantially higher rates of these injuries in states that have both PIP and no limitation on lawsuits. The data thus indicate that other factors are more important than PIP availability in explaining hard-to-verify injury claim patterns.

If the availability of general damages does cause individuals to file claims for nonexistent injuries, we should observe increases in hard-to-verify claims following the repeal no-fault. In fact, we do indeed observe increases in the proportion of claims with hard-to-verify injuries in both Georgia and Connecticut following their repeals of no-fault.[30] However, it is difficult to distinguish increases that may come from fraud from background increases in claim rates that occurred generally across the nation during this period.

As an alternative test, we examine claim rates in states with a choice system, comparing individuals who have elected to be covered under a verbal threshold to those retaining broader access to the tort system. An advantage of comparisons of this sort is that we are able to hold fixed state-specific factors that may otherwise vary when we look across states, such as the road infrastructure, driving laws, and availability of secondary insurers. Our analysis of the prevailing data on accident rates suggests that no-fault does not exert a causal effect on driving behavior, so any differences in hard-to-verify claims that we observe across those under no-fault and tort likely represent the incentive effects of the liability system.

Figure 5.8 plots claim rates for hard-to-verify injuries in New Jersey and Pennsylvania. New Jersey initially operated under a dollar-threshold system, but the thresholds were so low ($200 initially, with a $1,500 threshold option introduced later) that, in practice, few cases were excluded from the tort system. In 1989, New Jersey introduced a verbal threshold option limiting lawsuits to cases involving statutorily defined serious injury. The figure compares hard-to-verify claim rates among those selecting the verbal threshold to those without lawsuit

---

[30] In particular, between 1987 and 1997, the incidence of hard-to-verify injuries rose from 65 percent to 76 percent in Georgia and 56 percent to 75 percent in Connecticut.

**Figure 5.8**
**Trends in Soft-Tissue Claims**

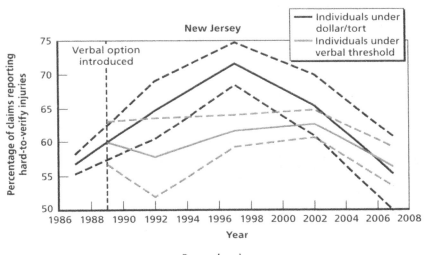

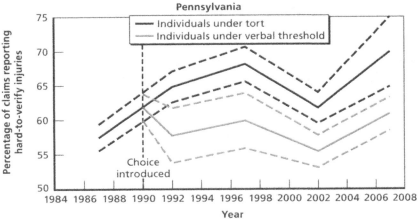

SOURCE: Authors' calculations from IRC closed-claim data (All-Industry Research Advisory Council, 1989b; IRC, 1993, 2003, 2008b).
NOTE: Dotted lines denote 95% confidence intervals for our estimates.
RAND *MG860-5.8*

limitations. PIP was required for both groups, so the differences across groups most likely represent the effects of access to general damages, not PIP. Consistent with our findings looking across states, we find a lower incidence of hard-to-verify injuries among those who elected a verbal threshold, with 8–10 percent fewer claims reporting such injuries during the 1990s.[31] Among those not limiting lawsuits, hard-to-verify claims dropped appreciably between 1997 and 2002, yielding comparable rates for full-tort and verbal-threshold claimants by the end of our sample.

Similar patterns were identified in Pennsylvania (see Figure 5.8). Pennsylvania required PIP coverage throughout the sample period for all motorists but introduced a choice system in 1990 that permitted owners to opt for a traditional tort system or a verbal threshold. Hard-to-verify injuries occurred in 6–8 percent fewer claims among those without access to general damages, and these differences persisted across the sample period. Overall, there is strong evidence both across and within states that access to general damages is associated with higher claiming rates for hard-to-verify injuries. Although the patterns we have documented in this section could conceivably arise due to unobserved differences in vehicle characteristics or driving behavior by those covered under no-fault, fraud appears to be a more reasonable explanation. The data also suggest that the prevalence of suspicious claims grew more quickly in no-fault states in the 1990s than it did in tort states.

We summarize the findings of this section by noting that claiming patterns depend on the incentives created by the insurance system and that the systems vary in the incentives they provide. Dollar-threshold no-fault, for example, encourages overclaiming around threshold points that is not apparent in other systems, while both verbal- and dollar-threshold no-fault appear to discourage claiming of nonexistent injuries by limiting access to noneconomic damages. One common

---

[31] For the differences in the figure to reflect a selection effect, individuals who elect the verbal threshold would have to have private information—that is, information known to the individual but not known to the insurer—regarding their likelihood of sustaining soft-tissue injuries relative to other types of injuries. We regard this scenario as unlikely.

pattern we see across both categories of fraud indicators is an increase in prevalence of suspicious claims in no-fault states over time. In particular, there is some evidence that threshold overclaiming has increased since the 1980s in some no-fault states and that hard-to-verify injuries have become relatively more common in no-fault states in the 2000s than in the 1990s.

### Are Claims for Lost Work Higher Under No-Fault?

Individuals may file more or longer-duration claims for lost work under no-fault, which would tend to increase the costs of this system, other things being equal. Higher claimed work losses may represent superior coverage provided by no-fault, which compensates individuals for losses that would otherwise not be compensated under tort. Alternatively, the different nature of coverage provided by no-fault may induce individuals to exaggerate their amount of lost work time, a phenomenon demonstrated in other insurance settings.[32] Although insurers typically require some evidence of lost wages in support of wage claims (such as a statement from an employer), documentation requirements are often relatively minimal, and workers have incentives to inflate their length of absence. However, it is not obvious whether no-fault systems are likely to generate stronger incentives to inflate work-loss claims.[33]

We first examine whether claims are more likely to report wage losses in no-fault states. Figure 5.9 plots the share of claimants reporting lost wages of any magnitude, by insurance regime. As in our previ-

---

[32] The strongest evidence of such overclaiming can be found in the workers' compensation literature, with numerous studies (e.g., Butler and Worrall, 1985; Meyer, Viscusi, and Durbin, 1995) demonstrating that generosity of benefits is correlated with length of absence following a work-related injury.

[33] A pure tort system may provide an incentive to inflate length of absence from work in order to increase general damages. However, even one-to-one wage reimbursement will generate incentives to malinger if victims would prefer not working to working. The greater certainty of reimbursement under a no-fault system may thus provide even stronger incentives for this type of overclaiming than are present in a tort system. Additionally, whereas both MedPay and PIP may generate incentives to report nonexistent injuries, MedPay provides no reimbursement for lost wages and thus would not encourage exaggeration of lost work.

**Figure 5.9**
**Trends in Claimed Wage Loss, by Insurance Regime**

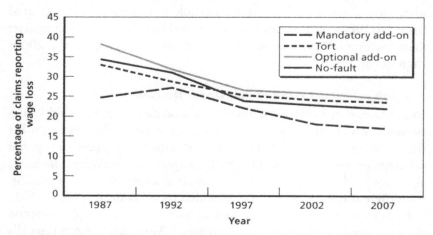

SOURCE: Authors' calculations from IRC closed-claim data (All-Industry Research
Advisory Council, 1989b; IRC, 1993, 2003, 2008b).
RAND MG860-5.9

ous analysis, we regression-adjust these rates to account for differences in driver, vehicle, and accident characteristics across states.[34]

Figure 5.9 shows that wage-loss claims have become less common over time across all insurance regimes. With the exception of a slightly lower rate of wage-loss claiming in mandatory–add-on states, the shares of claimants reporting wage losses are similar across insurance regimes.

We next examine whether claims for lost work time are larger in no-fault states. Figure 5.10 plots the average number of days of lost work claimed for those reporting lost wages, both over time and across insurance regime. As in Figure 5.9, we adjust our estimates to control for differences in characteristics of drivers, accidents, and injuries.[35] In tort states, average work losses have ranged between a high

---

[34] Here, the dependent variable is an indicator for whether a claim included lost wages, and the adjustment approach and set of control variables are identical to those used for Figure 5.7. Regression results are available from the authors.

[35] Here, our dependent variable is the number of days of lost work time, which is modeled as a function of the insurance regime and the set of control covariates listed earlier. Because

**Figure 5.10**
**Trends in Claimed Lost Work Time, by Insurance Regime**

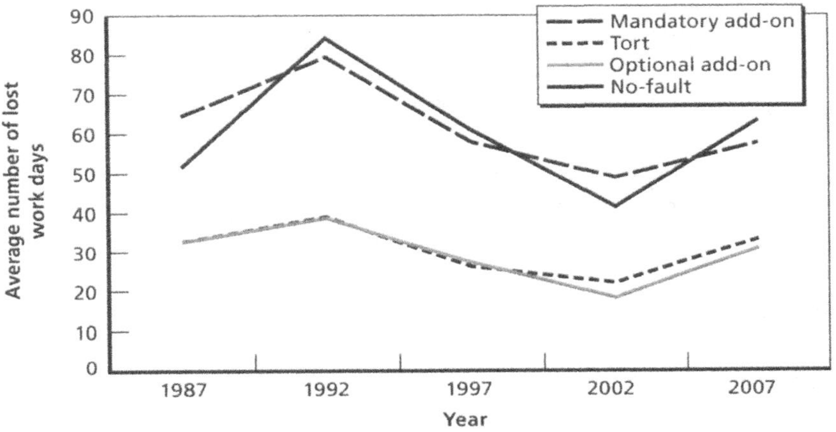

SOURCE: Authors' calculations from IRC closed-claim data (All-Industry Research Advisory Council, 1989b; IRC, 1993, 2003, 2008b).
RAND MG860-5.10

of 39 days in 1992 and a low of 22 days in 2002. Elective–add-on states look similar to tort states in both levels and trajectory over time. For mandatory–add-on and no-fault states, reported lost days of work are roughly double those of tort states in all years. These differences cannot reflect differences in accident or injury severity, since we control for these factors in our regressions. The fact that mandatory–add-on states behave similarly to no-fault states suggests that this pattern arises due to the generous nature of first-party PIP as opposed to the restrictions on access to tort. During the 1990s, claimed work losses were significantly above levels prevailing in the mid-1980s in no-fault states, although levels moderated somewhat in later sample years.

Although the evidence in Figure 5.10 suggests that PIP increases claimed lost work time, our analysis does not rule out other factors that may differ across PIP and other states that may explain such patterns,

___

these count data are highly skewed, our regressions were estimated using negative binomial regression, and the adjusted values were constructed by transforming the estimated coefficients into marginal effects at the means of the independent variables.

such as the quality of the workers' compensation system. However, similar patterns emerge within states. Figure 5.11 compares reported work-time losses in PIP and BI claims in Oregon.

We focus on Oregon because it is the largest mandatory–add-on state; for a given accident, a victim can choose whether to file a first-party PIP claim, a third-party claim, both, or neither. We would expect average lost work days in PIP claims to be equal to or lower than the average for BI claims, since more-costly accidents would exceed typical PIP policy limits and would thus require a third-party claim. However, the opposite is, in fact, true: In all years, the median reported lost work for PIP claims is equal to or above that for BI claims.[36] Given that other factors, such as the presence of alternative insurance providers, were likely relatively stable in this state, PIP availability provides the

**Figure 5.11**
**Trends in Lost Work, by Insurance Type in Oregon**

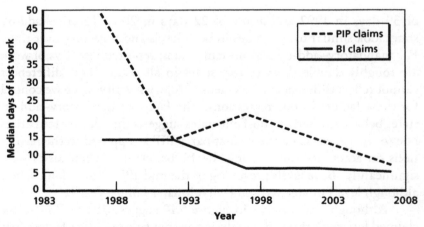

SOURCE: Authors' calculations from IRC closed-claim data (All-Industry Research Advisory Council, 1989b; IRC, 1993, 2003, 2008b).
RAND MG860-5.11

---

[36] We see similar patterns in elective add-on states, such as Texas, although, in these states, the higher number of claimed days may reflect selection into the purchase of PIP.

most reasonable explanation for the observed differences in claiming behavior.[37]

To summarize, we find evidence that the average number of days in lost-work claims is larger in states requiring PIP, including no-fault states. However, the differences in lost-work claiming between no-fault states and tort states have remained relatively stable over time. Thus, while lost-work claiming can explain differences in cost levels across systems, it provides a less plausible explanation for changes in relative costs over time. Our data do not permit us to determine whether the higher claiming under no-fault represents exaggeration of lost work time or more-complete claiming for actual losses.

### Does No-Fault Provide Different Levels of Reimbursement for Noneconomic Damages?

Critics of no-fault argue that a major limitation of the system is the denial of compensation for noneconomic losses to those whose injuries fall below the recovery threshold. Other things being equal, we expect that a lower level of payments for noneconomic losses will reduce costs and premiums, potentially counteracting some of the other factors we have already identified that make no-fault more expensive. Additionally, we expect that changes over time in the extent to which insurers in no-fault states provided compensation for noneconomic losses will affect the cost differences between no-fault and other systems.

To examine trends in payments for noneconomic losses over time, we used the IRC closed-claim data to calculate the aggregate total payments and the aggregate payments for general damages across insurance types in each survey year, and took the ratio of these aggregates to estimate the total share of payments that were made for noneconomic losses.[38] Assuming that the claims in the closed-claim data are representative, the ratio provides a measure of the extent to which expendi-

---

[37] In the closed-claim data, both Georgia and Connecticut also experienced declines in reported missed work after they repealed no-fault.

[38] We limited our analysis to BI, PIP, and MedPay claims with complete and coherent information about payments. All compensation provided by PIP and MedPay was considered as representing payments for economic losses.

tures are driven by costs not directly related to treatment.[39] Payment shares for noneconomic losses are plotted in Figure 5.12.[40]

The figure demonstrates that the share of compensation devoted to noneconomic losses was lower in no-fault states in 1987 than in

**Figure 5.12**
**Trends in Expenditures for Noneconomic Damages, by Insurance System**

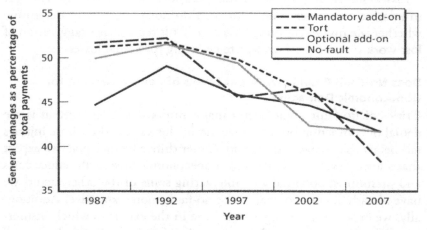

SOURCE: Authors' calculations from IRC closed-claim data (All-Industry Research Advisory Council, 1989b; IRC, 1993, 2003, 2008b).
RAND MG860-5.12

---

[39] The analysis here cannot speak to the equitability of payments for noneconomic damages across systems, because judging equitability would require information regarding the actual extent of noneconomic losses incurred by victims, regardless of whether these losses were reimbursed. We are not aware of data sources that provide such information.

[40] One potential concern with these calculations is that, given that each year's sample is drawn from claims sampled within a two-week window, exceptional claims that were settled within the sample window might disproportionately influence our results. To test for this possibility and obtain an indication of the variability of the claims arising due to the sampling scheme, we bootstrapped our estimates by randomly drawing from each year's claims with replacement. (*Replacement* is a statistical term describing how our bootstrapping procedure worked: Once a random draw was selected, it was not disqualified from selection again in later draws.) The estimated ratios are fairly precisely estimated and indicate that the decline in noneconomic damages over time in tort states and the change in the disparity between no-fault and tort states are statistically significant.

tort and add-on states, as would be expected if the limitation on law-suits under no-fault was successful in removing some cases from the courts.[41] However, over time, there has been a gradual convergence between no-fault and tort states, such that insurers under both systems were devoting the same share of payments to compensate noneconomic damages by 2007: 42 percent. Our finding that noneconomic-damage payments have fallen in tort states is consonant with the declining rate of litigation for these states documented in Figure 5.8. The fact that noneconomic damages have declined in importance for tort and add-on states while not diminishing in importance in no-fault states provides a further explanation for the increase in no-fault's costs, com-pared with those of other systems, over time.

### Does No-Fault Encourage Greater Claiming of Medical Services?

Medical costs represent a sizable portion of the total costs of PIP and BI claims, so differences in the use of medical services that are billed to auto insurers across states under different systems could explain much of the cost differences we document in Figures 4.1–4.6 in Chapter Four.

The medical costs borne by auto insurance (as opposed to health insurance or the victim) are influenced by the rules that govern priority of recovery and subrogation. When a person is injured in an automo-bile accident, there are often multiple sources from which the injured or his or her medical provider might be able to recover. For example, the victim might be able to recover from his or her own health insur-ance, workers' compensation (if the driving was job-related), his or her own no-fault PIP auto insurance, one or more tortfeasors, or their third-party BI insurers. The priority-of-recovery rules in each state will determine who is responsible. This is established by a combination of statute, insurance-policy language, and case law. In general, workers' compensation policies pay first, followed by no-fault automobile poli-cies and then other sources, including health insurance. Because no-

---

[41] Estimates and standard errors for this figure are available in the appendix.

fault plans usually have a higher priority than health insurance, they are more likely to bear the medical costs of an auto accident.[42]

Subrogation also affects the flow of funds following an accident and whether the losses are covered by auto insurance or another source. Subrogation is the adjustment of rights that occurs when a victim is entitled to recover from two sources, one of which bears primary legal responsibility. If the secondary source (often an insurer) pays the victim, it "steps into the shoes" of the victim and assumes the victim's legal rights against the party primarily responsible (often the tortfeasor). Accordingly, the insurer can recover against the tortfeasor.[43]

In the auto-insurance context, the existence of subrogation may affect who ultimately bears the loss. Suppose, for example, that a victim is injured in an automobile accident caused by driver x and that the victim has medical insurance and a viable suit against driver x. The medical provider that helps the victim bills the first-party health insurer. If the first-party medical insurer has the right of subrogation, it may be able to shift the cost of the automobile accident to driver x's BI insurance. If there is no subrogation, who ultimately bears the loss may simply depend on the happenstance of whether the medical provider billed the victim's medical insurer or driver x's BI insurer.

How does this affect relative costs of tort and no-fault? Because no-fault PIP insurance usually has a higher priority than health insur-

---

[42] Interestingly, two key proponents of no-fault, Robert Keeton and Jeffrey O'Connell, originally proposed making PIP secondary to health insurance. In their original proposal, auto insurance would cover on those expenses left uncovered by health insurance. Auto insurers fought this plan, however, fearing that health insurers would essentially swallow their entire business. Today, Michigan and New Jersey allow insureds to have the option of making their health insurance the primary payer, in exchange for a reduction in rates (O'Connell, 2008). According to one insurance-company executive with whom we spoke, health insurers in Michigan have reacted by excluding injuries from auto accidents in their policies— thus restoring the primacy of auto insurance in bearing automobile accident–related medical costs.

[43] The conventional policy justification for subrogation is to prevent the unjust enrichment of and double recovery by a victim. If the victim's loss is already covered, it makes no sense to permit him or her to recover from insurance. Some have also suggested that allowing insurance companies to recover the excess enables them to recycle that excess and pass it on to consumers in the form of lower premiums (Fleming, 1966, p. 1481; *Frost v. Porter Leasing Corp.*, 386 Mass. 425, 436 N.E.2d 387, 1982).

ance or tort BI insurance, it is more likely to end up bearing medical costs that are auto-accident related. Thus, in no-fault states, auto insurance almost certainly pays for a larger proportion of auto accident–related medical costs than in tort states, where first-party medical insurance pays for a higher proportion.

There is a second reason that medical costs may be higher in no-fault states. Automobile insurers have suggested that no-fault insurance has become an especially attractive payer to health-care providers because it pays a much higher percentage of billed medical costs than medical insurance, which usually includes steep discounts.[44] As medical costs have increased during the past two decades, no-fault automobile insurance was virtually the only insurer that paid the provider's full bill. Thus, medical providers were much more likely to initially bill no-fault insurance prior to seeking recovery against the victim's medical insurance. In tort states, in contrast, medical providers sought reimbursement from the medical insurers, which then may or may not eventually seek reimbursement from the BI auto insurer, depending on the status of the slower-moving third-party claim. This, they argue, has led to increased costs of first-party automobile insurance.[45]

To address this issue of claimed medical costs, we examine the closed-claim data. In this section, we measure claimed medical use by first looking at the likelihood of a claimant utilizing a particular category of medical provider. We then look at the intensity of care by comparing the average number of visits to each category of medical provider. On both these metrics, we find that the data show sizable dif-

---

[44] Interview with auto insurer, June 2007. One reason for this discrepancy has to do with the business model of auto insurers, which focuses less attention on medical-claim management than does the health insurers' model. Additionally, in many no-fault states, auto insurers are explicitly barred by statute or regulation from entering into managed-care arrangements with medical providers.

[45] The Colorado experience is illuminating. After the repeal of no-fault, average auto-insurance premiums dropped 35 percent between July 2003 and December 2007 (BBC Research and Consulting, 2008, p. 5). In contrast, the costs of inpatient medical care resulting from motor-vehicle accidents shifted from no-fault to Medicare, Medicaid, and the victims (BBC Research and Consulting, 2008, p. 10). Hospitals reported that reimbursement rates fell from 60 percent in 2002 to just 36 percent in 2006 after the repeal of no-fault. EMS providers were affected in similar ways (BBC Research and Consulting, 2008, p. 12).

ferences in the use of medical services. Claimed medical care is higher in no-fault states than in tort states.

## How Likely Is a Claimant to Use a Particular Category of Medical Provider?

Table 5.8 reports the proportion of claimants who claimed particular types of medical care, by year and insurance system, adjusting for differences in accident, injury, vehicle, and driver characteristics across states.[46] As one can see from this table, no-fault regimes are associated

---

[46] Because we are interested primarily in understanding how medical care contributes to cost of insurance, we focus on care in accidents that result in filed claims. We obtain similar findings to those reported in this section from the consumer panel data, which does not require us to confine attention to accidents with filed claims.

Although the analysis in this section includes the most-common forms of treatment, there are a number of other types of treatment that may represent important cost drivers that we leave unexamined. Insurance-industry representatives have claimed that an important new dimension contributing to medical costs is the utilization of alternative treatment providers, such as herbalists, hypnotherapists, and aromatherapists. Unfortunately, the closed-claim data contain data on such alternative treatments only for later years, and the utilization of such providers is sufficiently infrequent in our sample that we are unable to draw strong conclusions about how such treatments may influence costs. Further research is warranted examining both how the supply of such alternative physicians differs across states and how the insurance system affects their utilization.

To construct Table 5.8, we estimated probit regressions of a 0-1 indicator for whether or not a claimant used a particular type of medical provider on indicators for whether a claim was subject to no-fault, optional add-on, or mandatory add-on provisions, with tort as the excluded category. The unit of observation was a claim. Additional control variables included fixed effects for the hour, number of vehicles, and location type of the accident (five categories); impact severity (six categories); injury severity (six categories); claimant age (five-year intervals), sex, marital status, seat position, and seat-belt use; coverage limits of the insured (eight categories); and separate indicators for no injury, burns, serious lacerations, scarring, neck sprains or strains, back sprains or strains, other sprains of strains, fracture of weight-bearing bone, other types of fractures, organ damage, concussion, permanent brain injury, loss of body part, paralysis, temporomandibular-joint injury, loss of senses, fatality, other injury, and unknown injury. Choice states were excluded from the sample. The regressions were separately estimated for each survey year. The table was constructed by adding the proportion of claimants in tort states using a particular type of medical provider to the appropriately transformed probit regression coefficient estimates for each insurance type. The 34 regressions estimated for the table and the covariates included in each regression are available from the authors upon request. The set of provider types reported in the table represent all of the provider types that were consistently reported across years in the closed-claim data.

**Table 5.8**
**Percentage of Victims Utilizing Particular Medical Services, by Insurance Regime and Year**

| Type of Treatment | Year | Liability System | | | |
| | | Tort | No-Fault | Mandatory Add-On | Optional Add-On |
| --- | --- | --- | --- | --- | --- |
| ER visit | 1987 | 32.4 | 47.2** | 43.9** | 38.5** |
| | 1992 | 35.1 | 44.7** | 38.3 | 38.3** |
| | 1997 | 44.4 | 47.5** | 43.7 | 43.7 |
| | 2002 | 44.9 | 46.9** | 39.3** | 45.5 |
| | 2007 | 47.1 | 48.7 | 41.9** | 48.8* |
| Overnight hospital stay | 1987 | 8.95 | 10.3** | 9.64 | 9.56* |
| | 1992 | 6.53 | 7.21** | 5.87 | 6.84 |
| | 1997 | 5.35 | 5.57 | 5.88 | 5.22 |
| | 2002 | 5.44 | 6.34** | 5.15 | 5.18 |
| | 2007 | 4.52 | 5.09** | 4.06 | 4.64 |
| Visit to chiropractor | 1987 | 13.3 | 15.4** | 14.5 | 10.2** |
| | 1992 | 21.4 | 25.8** | 19.1* | 17.5** |
| | 1997 | 30.6 | 33.8** | 32.0 | 25.4** |
| | 2002 | 32.7 | 34.3* | 26.6** | 27.9** |
| | 2007 | 31.5 | 37.3** | 28.4* | 30.3 |
| Visit to physical therapist | 1987 | 7.18 | 6.95 | 10.5** | 10.3** |
| | 1992 | 12.3 | 13.0 | 16.5** | 17.3** |
| | 1997 | 15.7 | 21.3** | 25.4** | 22.0** |
| | 2002 | 16.0 | 27.1** | 26.0** | 20.5** |
| | 2007 | 13.4 | 22.9** | 27.6** | 18.0** |
| Visit to dentist | 1987 | 1.09 | 1.34** | 0.880 | 1.28** |
| | 1992 | 1.85 | 2.24* | 1.99 | 1.71 |
| | 1997 | 1.58 | 1.88** | 1.45 | 1.54 |

**Table 5.8—Continued**

| Type of Treatment | Year | Tort | No-Fault | Mandatory Add-On | Optional Add-On |
|---|---|---|---|---|---|
| | | | **Liability System** | | |
| Visit to dentist (continued) | 2002 | 1.11 | 1.84** | 1.05 | 1.13 |
| | 2007 | n.a. | n.a. | n.a. | n.a. |
| Visit to psychotherapist | 1987 | 0.716 | 0.816* | 0.822 | 0.691 |
| | 1992 | 1.19 | 2.02** | 1.01 | 1.33 |
| | 1997 | 0.567 | 1.82** | 0.840 | 0.566 |
| | 2002 | 0.494 | 2.61** | 0.542 | 0.526 |
| | 2007 | 0.351 | 1.23** | 0.335 | 0.327 |
| None | 1987 | 3.06 | 2.47** | 2.77** | 2.98* |
| | 1992 | 3.09 | 1.78** | 2.75 | 3.06 |
| | 1997 | 7.39 | 5.63** | 6.44** | 7.40 |
| | 2002 | 10.3 | 8.50** | 11.9* | 11.0* |
| | 2007 | 9.78 | 6.69** | 7.61** | 9.09* |

SOURCE: Authors' calculations from IRC closed-claim data (All-Industry Research Advisory Council, 1989b; IRC, 1993, 2003, 2008b).

* = statistically significantly different from the value for tort states at the 5% level.

** = statistically significantly different from the value for tort states at the 1% level.

with greater likelihoods of an accident victim visiting almost every category of health-care provider in almost every year for which we have data.[47]

Trends in claimed ER use differ substantially across systems. In all years, claimed ER use is more common in no-fault states than in tort states. An increasing share of patients has accessed the emergency

---

[47] We also conducted this analysis without controlling for accident, injury, vehicle, and driver characteristics and obtained generally similar results, although, for some types of treatment, such as emergency room (ER) utilization, differences across regimes were even more pronounced. This suggests not only that otherwise-similar individuals consume more treatment in no-fault states but also that no-fault states have more of the types of people who consume certain types of costly treatment.

department in tort states over time, while, in absolute terms, ER claiming has been stable in no-fault and add-on states. ER care can likely explain some of the higher costs observed in no-fault states in the mid-1980s, but, over time, ER-care trends have actually promoted convergence across systems.

There is also a higher claimed usage of many types of specialized physicians in no-fault states, in comparison to both tort states and add-on states. The claimed use of chiropractors and physical therapists has grown over time across all states. However, the growth in physical-therapist use has been particularly striking in no-fault states, with an additional 16 percent of claimants utilizing these services in 2007 relative to 1987. Dental utilization has remained stable across time for all groups but is higher among no-fault claimants. For psychotherapists, utilization among victims in tort and add-on states has been low and relatively stable over time. In no-fault states, utilization has risen. Interestingly, for all types of states, there has been an increase over time in the proportion of claimants who report no medical care, but this proportion is slightly lower among those under no-fault. In short, we see that claimants from no-fault states are more likely to use nearly every category of medical provider than claimants from tort states.

By comparing the differences between no-fault and mandatory–add-on states, we can contrast the effects of first-party insurance (PIP) with the effects of limiting access to the tort system. For the more common types of care, such as physical therapists and chiropractors, utilization rates in mandatory–add-on states are comparable to those in no-fault states. However, for rarer types of treatment, such as dentistry, psychotherapy, and overnight hospital visits, utilization among no-fault patients is higher. Although we control for policy-limit bands in our analysis, one possibility is that these differences reflect the generally higher policy limits for PIP in no-fault states. Because there are relatively few individuals in add-on states with very high coverages, our controls may not perfectly capture differences in policy limits. Minimum required PIP benefits in Delaware and Oregon (add-on states) are relatively generous at $15,000 per person, but these benefits are still small relative to the PIP benefits available in many no-fault states.

Table 5.8 also sheds light on our previous finding that BI costs dropped substantially in tort states during the 1990s. Given the enormous increases in medical costs during this period, a fall in BI costs was unexpected. However, Table 5.8 demonstrates large increases in the number of individuals who received no medical treatment and significant drops in the share of patients consuming the most expensive form of treatment: an overnight hospital stay during the sample period. Thus, even though treatment costs were rising, substitution toward less expensive forms of treatment or no treatment helped to rein in costs. These changes were also not unique to tort states but are observed to some extent across all systems.

Overall, Table 5.8 suggests that higher medical utilization was an important contributor to the higher costs of no-fault. Claimants in no-fault states were more likely to use almost all types of care, including that of specialized physicians. For physical therapy and psychotherapy, no-fault states have also increased utilization at a faster rate than other states.

### How Many Visits to a Medical Provider Is a Victim Likely to Claim?

In addition to examining types of providers, we examine treatment intensity by using data on the claimed number of visits made to various providers. Besides using more-specialized types of medical providers, victims covered by no-fault make more visits to these providers.

Table 5.9 reports adjusted average counts of doctor visits, conditional on making at least one visit, by insurance system.[48] Average numbers of visits were falling over time for all physician types and all liability systems, providing further evidence that reductions in treatment can explain the liability-premium declines in tort and add-on states during the 1990s.

The largest difference between insurance regimes is seen among chiropractors, with a typical no-fault patient making ten additional

---

[48] Adjustments are made using negative binomial regressions to account for the discrete count nature of the data, and the same set of control variables used in Figure 5.7 are used in this analysis. The regressions used to construct the table are available from the authors upon request. Unadjusted comparisons yield similar results. The closed-claim surveys did not collect data on number of visits prior to 1992.

**Table 5.9**
**Average Number of Claimed Visits Among Those Using a Particular**
**Provider Type, by Insurance Regime and Year**

| Number of Visits | Year | Liability System | | | |
|---|---|---|---|---|---|
| | | Tort | No-Fault | Mandatory Add-On | Optional Add-On |
| Osteopath | 1992 | 9.57 | 10.1 | 8.19 | 8.78 |
| | 1997 | 9.40 | 10.2 | 11.1 | 8.62 |
| | 2002 | 6.70 | 8.70* | 4.95 | 7.81 |
| | 2007 | 6.45 | 6.06 | 7.89 | 7.00 |
| Chiropractor | 1992 | 23.8 | 34.1** | 23.0 | 23.2 |
| | 1997 | 21.8 | 32.9** | 22.1 | 20.8** |
| | 2002 | 20.6 | 29.1** | 23.5** | 19.3** |
| | 2007 | 18.8 | 27.5** | 23.5** | 19.8* |
| Physical therapist | 1992 | 18.1 | 22.9** | 21.6* | 16.6** |
| | 1997 | 15.0 | 21.9** | 16.8* | 14.3 |
| | 2002 | 13.7 | 22.5** | 15.2 | 12.8* |
| | 2007 | 13.2 | 21.3** | 15.8* | 13.4 |
| Dentist | 1992 | 8.92 | 8.12 | 10.7 | 7.56 |
| | 1997 | 3.15 | 4.87** | 3.64 | 3.50 |
| | 2002 | 2.92 | 4.31** | 3.85 | 2.94 |
| | 2007 | n.a. | n.a. | n.a. | n.a. |
| Psychotherapist | 1992 | 11.1 | 11.3 | 8.43 | 13.7 |
| | 1997 | 8.78 | 11.7** | 9.37 | 6.78 |
| | 2002 | 7.62 | 7.99 | 3.83 | 8.17 |
| | 2007 | 8.00 | 8.49 | 4.11* | 6.20 |

SOURCE: Authors' calculations from IRC closed-claim data (All-Industry Research Advisory Council, 1989b; IRC, 1993, 2003, 2008b).

* = statistically significantly different from the value for tort states at the 5% level.

** = statistically significantly different from the value for tort states at the 1% level.

visits, a difference that has remained relatively stable over time. Although individuals under no-fault are only slightly more likely to see a chiropractor, overall use of chiropractic services is thus substantially higher under a no-fault regime.

Another notable difference across systems concerns use of physical therapists: Whereas the average number of therapist visits declined by roughly five visits per claim in tort and add-on states between 1992 and 2007, it remained stable in no-fault states. A similar pattern is observable in dentistry, for which tort and add-on states have seen larger declines in the number of claimed visits than no-fault states.[49] For osteopathy and psychotherapy, intensity of use appears more similar across different types of states.

The variations in utilization we document may reflect higher patient demand for certain types of care in PIP states, the effect of medical providers billing PIP more than BI, or the actions of organized fraud rings. We are skeptical of the fraud explanation for several reasons. Many of the differences in utilization are apparent in the early 1990s, a period in which there is less evidence of organized fraud in PIP. Also, our interviews with fraud-detection experts suggest that organized rings tend to submit claims involving a wide variety of doctors, but our measures of utilization of different types of physicians are no more correlated in no-fault states than they are in tort states. In other words, claimants in no-fault states are no more likely to use many different types of doctors than claimants in tort states.

An obvious question is whether the increased claimed medical care documented in Tables 5.8 and 5.9 is evidence that no-fault is working as planned, evidence of waste and fraud, or evidence that medical providers are more likely to bill PIP than BI. On the one hand, we might expect victims under no-fault to appropriately use more medical care. One of the arguments proponents of no-fault made was that some victims under tort systems did not receive adequate medical care because they could not afford it and struggled to recover their medical expenses from third-party insurers. For those endorsing no-fault, no-

---

[49] Other commentators have also noted the greater use of alternative providers in no-fault states (see, e.g, Kinzler, 2006, p. 23).

fault's higher medical costs are evidence that it is working to provide more care for victims of automobile accidents.

On the other hand, critics of no-fault argue that no-fault's higher medical costs are simply the result of waste and fraud and no-fault's general failure to introduce cost controls that are used by first-party medical insurers. Unfortunately, our data cannot answer this important question, and further research is necessary. In particular, research addressing the interaction of health and auto insurance is necessary to understand the way in which the choice of auto-insurance regime affects health-insurance costs.

### Is Medical Cost Inflation Different in No-Fault States?

As explained in the preceding section, victims under no-fault regimes claim the use of more medical care—they are more likely to visit medical providers and visit more often. But we also find that the medical care in no-fault states is more expensive and has grown more expensive over time. These cost differences may reflect factors unrelated to the auto-insurance system, such as diffusion of medical technology or changes in the competitive structure of the health-care industry that vary by state. No-fault itself may also directly affect costs by affecting physician billing practices or allowing providers to achieve economies of scale in certain types of care.[50] Regardless of the cause, we find that medical costs grew substantially more quickly in no-fault states.

A simple way to examine medical cost inflation would be to compare indexes of medical costs in states under different insurance systems over time. Unfortunately, such time-varying state-level medical cost indexes are not available. We adopt an alternative approach to measuring cost trends that utilizes our claim data. For each patient in our sample, we can calculate the expected medical charges based on injuries, treatment received, and demographic characteristics, under the assumption that charging patterns follow national averages. We can then examine whether actual charges are higher than these expected

---

[50] For example, some of our interviewees claimed anecdotally that no-fault charges were used to fund the operation of several large trauma centers in the Denver, Colorado, area.

charges in no-fault states and whether any differences have diminished or augmented over time.[51]

Table 5.10 reports adjusted median costs for medical treatment in tort states over time, along with cost ratios by insurance system and survey year. Costs are measured relative to tort states and thus indicate the degree to which costs for similar patients were higher or lower in states with alternative insurance systems. For example, the first no-fault entry of 5.86 percent means that, when comparing medical charges for two individuals with identical injuries, demographic characteristics, and utilization of treatment, one of whom lived in a tort state in 1987 and one of whom lived in a no-fault state, on average, we expect the individual in the no-fault state to report expenses that are 5.86 percent higher.[52] Given that the price of medical care was generally rising during this period, it is unsurprising to observe that the median cost of care in tort states rose between 1987 and 2007, conditional on injury and treatment.

Table 5.10 documents an enormous increase in relative medical costs in no-fault states during the 1990s. Prior to 1987, charges for individuals in no-fault states were only slightly higher (5.7 percent) than for comparably injured individuals in tort states. However, by 1997, the disparity had grown beyond 40 percent.[53] Although there

---

[51] Specifically, for each survey year, we estimated a claim-level linear regression model in which the dependent variable was the log of claimed medical expenses and the primary explanatory variables were indicators for whether a claim was subject to no-fault, optional add-on, or mandatory add-on provisions, with tort as the excluded category. The additional variables used in constructing Figure 5.7 were included as controls along with indicators for no treatment, overnight hospital treatment, ER treatment, and treatment by chiropractors, dentists, psychologists, and physical therapists. Choice states and states that changed insurance regimes between 1987 and 2007 were excluded from the sample.

[52] Although we think of these differences as primarily representing actual differences in medical costs, it is also possible that some of the patterns evident in Table 5.10 represent fraud. Because we control for injury severity, we adjust for the possibility of differential claiming for nonexistent injuries. However, fraud that takes the form of submitting claims for actual injuries but reporting charges in excess of the actual cost of treatment will affect the numbers reported in Table 5.10.

[53] In attempting to explain the enormous variation in medical costs among otherwise-similar communities, Atul Gawande (2009) recently argued that the centrality of profit maximization in the local medical culture may be the most plausible explanation. By providing a

**Table 5.10**
**Cost of Medical Care in States with Other Insurance Regimes, Relative to Tort States**

| Survey Year | Median Cost of Care in Tort States ($) | Cost of Care Relative to Tort States (%) | | |
|---|---|---|---|---|
| | | No-Fault States | Mandatory Add-On States | Optional Add-On States |
| 1987 | 972 | 5.86 | −10.50 | −11.44 |
| 1992 | 1,758 | 25.76 | −12.92 | −5.91 |
| 1997 | 1,414 | 51.06 | −11.19 | 6.75 |
| 2002 | 1,584 | 50.43 | −14.92 | 3.35 |
| 2007 | 1,936 | 42.90 | −6.17 | −3.50 |

SOURCE: Authors' calculations from IRC closed-claim data (All-Industry Research Advisory Council, 1989b; IRC, 1993, 2003, 2008b).

NOTE: All relative differences except those in mandatory–add-on states in 2007 are statistically significant at the 5% level (see shading). Dollar costs are expressed in year 2000 dollars.

was some relative cost growth in optional–add-on states, growth was much smaller in these states, and there is no evidence of growth in mandatory–add-on states. This evidence of high medical cost inflation reaffirms the patterns in Figure 4.1 in Chapter Four, which showed a growing premium-cost gap between no-fault states and states with other insurance systems between 1987 and 2002. An important distinction, however, is that the analysis in Table 5.10 demonstrates that this differential growth persists even after accounting for interstate differences in auto injuries and victims' demographic characteristics. Rising costs under no-fault were not a matter simply of increased utilization of treatment but also of rising charges for the same treatment.

Does this medical inflation primarily reflect trends in the larger no-fault states? To explore this hypothesis, we differentiate the larger

---

source of payments that was not constrained by health-insurance scrutiny, no-fault may have provided an opportunity for doctors to enrich themselves—or to subsidize below-cost care for uninsured patients.

**Table 5.11**
**Differential Cost Patterns in Larger Versus Smaller No-Fault States (%)**

| Survey Year | Cost of Care Relative to Tort States | |
|---|---|---|
| | Small, Dollar-Threshold | Large, Verbal-Threshold |
| 1987 | 6.35 | 6.98 |
| 1992 | 14.03 | 24.68 |
| 1997 | 21.44 | 48.90 |
| 2002 | 17.18 | 52.57 |
| 2007 | 4.07 | 60.78 |

SOURCE: Authors' calculations from IRC closed-claim data (All-Industry Research Advisory Council, 1989b; IRC, 1993, 2003, 2008b).

NOTE: All differences except dollar-threshold states in 2007 are statistically significant at the 5% level (see shading).

verbal-threshold states (New York, Michigan, and Florida) from the smaller no-fault states in Table 5.11.[54]

We see an ever-widening gap between medical inflation in the smaller and larger no-fault states. In 1987, payments were 6–7 percent higher in both types of no-fault states than in tort states. Beginning in the early 1990s, medical cost inflation was substantially higher in the larger no-fault states. While even smaller no-fault states experienced higher costs than tort states through the 1990s, by 2002, costs had risen an additional 50 percent in the largest no-fault states. Interestingly, between 1997 and 2007, costs in dollar-threshold no-fault states converged toward those in tort states, while cost inflation continued in verbal-threshold states. Much of the overall difference in costs between larger and smaller no-fault states observed in Figure 4.6 in Chapter Four is likely attributable to this differential cost inflation.

---

[54] These cost differentials were constructed analogously to those reported in Table 5.10.

## Summary of Key Factors Behind Cost Growth

Why have claim costs been generally higher in no-fault states? In this chapter, we analyzed various data to determine the sources of these cost differences. We first consider and reject the possibility that no-fault causes more accidents than other systems. We also find that the likelihood of filing a claim after an accident is not any higher under no-fault than other regimes. Instead, we find that claims are more expensive under no-fault. Claimant reimbursement and satisfaction are slightly higher under no-fault, and no-fault appears to result in faster claim processing. These factors may contribute to higher claim and administrative costs. We found evidence of fraudulent activity under all regimes, but certain fraud indicators have risen over time in no-fault states. Additionally, litigation and insurer expenditures for non-economic damages have fallen over time in tort states while remaining stable in no-fault states.

The relative cost of no-fault grew primarily due to much higher medical costs. Individuals in no-fault states claimed the use of more medical care than claimants in other states. Physician visits billed to auto insurers have remained stable in no-fault states even as they fell in states with other insurance systems during the 1990s. Moreover, medical cost inflation skyrocketed in no-fault states.

But why, exactly, have medical claim costs grown so much faster in no-fault states? Anecdotally, stakeholders have suggested several reasons. First, as the practice of medicine has gotten more complex, the business of managing medical care to minimize costs has also grown enormously in complexity. Since PIP is a form of mandatory first-party medical insurance that covers one of the largest medical risks that a person faces, auto insurers are serving as medical insurers. But first-party health insurers have much more specialized expertise in doing this than auto insurers.

Second, stakeholders report that first-party health insurers have much more flexibility in writing contractual provisions that allow them to control costs. While first-party health insurance is regulated by state and federal agencies, health insurers have far more latitude than auto insurers, for which the relevant contracts are much more constrained by each state's automobile-insurance law and state regulators.

Finally, some auto insurers have cited the growth in bad-faith lawsuits as restricting their ability to investigate questionable claims under no-fault. Most states permit lawsuits by insureds against their own insurance companies for bad-faith failure to pay claims.[55] In such suits, the plaintiff alleges that the insurer violated its general duty of good faith in dealing with its insureds. In the early 1970s, the theory that the insurer must act in good faith was extended to a failure to reasonably pay first-party claims.[56] According to consumer advocates and plaintiffs' attorneys, insurers deliberately delay or withhold claim payments in order to increase profits and reduce costs (Stewart and Stewart, 2001, p. 33; Hunter, 2008; O'Connell, 2008). On this view, bad-faith insurance claims with punitive damages against the insurer are necessary to provide an adequate deterrent against this behavior and to remedy the economic imbalance between the insurance company and the insured (Mayerson, 2003, pp. 865–866). Insurance companies, however, argue that the fear of bad-faith claims prevents them from adequately investigating fraudulent no-fault claims. Bad-faith claims have grown in frequency and importance during the past 20 years (*Employees' Benefit Ass'n v. Grissett*, 732 So.2d 968, 978, Ala. 1998: "[O]nce thought to be a rarely applicable remedy, recovery for the tort of an insurer's bad faith failure to pay a claim appears now with great frequency"). By one

---

[55] E.g., Calif. Ins. Code §790.03(h); Colo. Rev. Stat. §10-3-1104(h); Conn Gen. Stat. §38a-321; 18 Del. Code §2304(16); Fla. Stat. §624.155; Ga. Code. §§33-6-34, 33-4-6; 431 Hawaii Statutes 13-102; 215 Ill. Comp. Stat. §5/155; Iowa Code §516.1; Mass. Gen. Law Ch. 93A §9, Ch. 176D, §3; Mo. Rev. Stat. §375.420; Mont. Code. §33-18-242; 42 Pa. Cons. Stat. §8371; R.I. Gen. Laws §9-1-33; Tenn. Code. §56-7-105; Texas Ins. Code. §21.21–2; Wisc. Admin. Code §6.11; Wisc. Stat. Ann. §632.22. In other states, the bad-faith cause of action is governed by common law. Important early cases include *Fletcher v. Western National Life Ins. Co.* (10 Cal. App. 3d 376, 1970), *Sukup v. State* (19 N.Y.2d 519, Ct. App., 1967), *Gruenberg v. Aetna Ins. Co.* (510 P.2d 1032, Cal. 1973), and *Anderson v. Continental Ins. Co.* (85 Wis. 2d 675, 1978).

[56] In *Gruenberg v. Aetna Ins. Co.* (Cal. 1973), the California Supreme Court first recognized a bad-faith claim when the insurer failed to pay the insured's first-party claim.

recent count, 27 states recognize a first-party bad-faith claim (Houser, Clark, and Bolduan, 2003–2004, p. 1048).[57]

Because damages from these suits can be quite high, no-fault insurers have greater incentives to pay quickly in order to avoid them. In contrast, bad-faith claims are not permitted in most tort states, since the defendant insurer is not that of the claimant. According to insurers, as bad-faith claims have become more common and more important, they have increasingly hindered efforts to vigorously investigate no-fault claims and comparatively increased the medical costs in no-fault states.

While all of these explanations are plausible, we lack data to confirm or refute them, and further research is necessary.

---

[57] There is evidence that indicates that insurers are more likely to settle claims for higher amounts when bad-faith claims are available to plaintiffs (Browne, Pryor, and Puelz, 2004). It is difficult to determine whether this is because insurance companies are simply settling legitimate claims more quickly and are appropriately deterred from stalling, or whether they do not have the time to investigate fraudulent claims that, absent the bad-faith law, they would otherwise investigate. According to one plaintiffs' attorney, bad-faith claims are potentially quite lucrative for plaintiffs, and insurers hire higher-quality outside counsel than they otherwise do in handling claims.

# CHAPTER SIX

# Conclusion, Policy Implications, and Future Developments

Almost from the time that automobile accidents emerged as a serious problem, critics of the tort approach to compensating victims for automobile accidents sought an alternative system. After more than 40 years of study, no-fault emerged in the early 1970s as a long-awaited solution to the problems identified with the tort system. At first, it appeared as though no-fault would prove to be a genuinely superior policy tool. Over time, however, the debate over automobile insurance shifted away from the problems with the tort system to focus on consumer premium cost and the right to sue dangerous drivers. Insurer and consumer-group support for no-fault waned.

We analyzed several data sources and concluded that the perception that no-fault generally had higher compensation costs than other regimes was largely accurate. Per-policy costs are highest in no-fault states, and these states have also experienced more-dramatic cost growth over time. Mandatory- and optional-add-on states also exhibit higher costs than tort states, but policy costs in these states still lag behind those of no-fault states, suggesting that no-fault itself, and not simply the availability of first-party PIP benefits, plays a role in differential costs.

We think that this has occurred for several reasons. Most importantly, individuals in no-fault states utilize more specialized types of treatment, and there is evidence of greater medical cost inflation in no-fault states. Physician visits have remained stable in no-fault states even as they fell in states with other insurance systems during the 1990s.

There is some evidence that no-fault's advantages in reducing litigation have decreased over time. Indicators of fraudulent claiming have also risen in no-fault states from their levels in the early 1990s. Thus, no-fault seems to have grown more expensive over time. This has led to a decline in support.

## Policy Lessons

Our central finding is that the recent decline in support for no-fault automobile insurance is the result of higher consumer premium costs stemming from increasing medical costs. What lessons should policy-makers draw from this?

### Is No-Fault a Failed Policy Experiment?

One obvious question this raises is whether no-fault is a policy experiment that has failed. We think that such a conclusion would be premature. Many of the problems identified with using the tort system to compensate automobile-accident victims by the original proponents of no-fault still exist. For example, there is no evidence that the well-documented disproportionality between a victim's economic loss and recovery in the tort system has been reduced. Nor is there evidence that tort is superior to no-fault in maximizing overall social welfare. No-fault has also been successful in reimbursing economic losses and reducing the time for payment of claims compared to tort states.

Moreover, focusing on the costs of automobile-insurance premiums alone obscures the ways in which auto-insurance systems may differ in costs shifted to other institutions. For example, no-fault states shift some of the costs of medical care for automobile accidents to auto insurance from medical insurance. In most no-fault states, medical providers bill no-fault auto insurance prior to other first-party medical insurance. In tort states, however, medical providers are more likely to bill first-party medical insurers. This effect may reduce health-insurance costs in no-fault states. Focusing solely on auto-insurance premium costs obscures a full accounting of the costs of the two systems.

One could also sketch a behavioral economic justification for no-fault automobile insurance. Human beings are notoriously poor at thinking about low-probability events like automobile accidents (Kunreuther, 1982, p. 209).[1] Research has long indicated that almost every driver believes that he or she is better than average, an obvious statistical impossibility (Svenson, 1981). Hence, drivers systematically underestimate the probability that they will be in an accident at all and underinsure against that risk. Drivers' rosy view of their driving ability also causes them to discount the possibility that they will be at fault in an accident. This causes them to underinsure against that possibility— the very benefit that no-fault auto insurance provides. In this way, mandated no-fault coverage can be justified as a form of paternalism that improves social welfare.[2]

There is also some evidence suggesting that a choice system may avoid some of the problems associated with conventional no-fault. For example, the no-fault component in Pennsylvania, a choice state, grew from 37 percent of drivers in 1993 to 53 percent of drivers in 2005, and insurers in this state have been able to offer no-fault rates at or below the regulatory guidelines. Although, on average, no-fault systems may have functioned less well during the 1990s, the increasing proportion of drivers selecting no-fault suggests that choice no-fault is popular in Pennsylvania.[3] Unfortunately, the number of choice states was too small to include in our primary analyses, so more research on choice states is necessary.

### How Could No-Fault Be Improved?

Because increased medical costs are largely responsible for the costs of no-fault, controlling those costs is critical to improving no-fault.

---

[1] People tend to underestimate the likelihood of a low-probability event until one occurs. At that point, we overestimate the likelihood of a similar event's recurrence. See also Mashaw and Harfst (1990, pp. 141–146), discussing the regulation of school buses in the wake of highly publicized school-bus accidents.

[2] See Liebman and Zeckhauser (2008), who argue that behavioral economics justify intervention in health-insurance markets.

[3] Only $5,000 of PIP is required in Pennsylvania. This low requirement distinguishes the Pennsylvania no-fault system from no-fault systems designed to cover catastrophic injuries.

Changing the default prioritization rules is one reform that appears promising.

In most no-fault states, medical providers bill no-fault insurance, if it is available, before billing any other source, including medical insurance. This means that auto insurers in no-fault states are essentially acting as medical insurers. Representatives of auto insurers to whom we spoke suggested that medical insurers are much better at managing care and tracking billing to reduce medical costs. Prioritizing first-party medical insurance over no-fault automobile insurance for medical costs appears a promising way of controlling auto accident–related medical costs.

There are also other promising approaches. Several states, including New York, Florida, New Jersey, and Pennsylvania, have adopted reimbursement schedules or other treatment restrictions in an effort to reduce medical costs for no-fault. Interstate comparisons of these efforts to control medical costs under PIP might show which approaches are most effective.

Policymakers could also reduce costs by decoupling first-party insurance and a limit on suits or noneconomic damages. The original vision of no-fault envisioned a generous PIP policy, justifying limited or ideally no access to the tort system. Add-on states decoupled these two by permitting or requiring PIP without restricting tort. The converse is also possible—limiting tort without requiring a PIP policy. In Pennsylvania, a choice state, consumers can receive a substantial discount on their automobile insurance in exchange for agreeing to accept a verbal threshold for access to the tort system. While first-party MedPay is required, the minimum policy is a relatively modest $5,000. Many consumers have elected the limited-tort option in exchange for a reduction of their rates. Permitting consumers to elect to limit noneconomic damages without requiring first-party insurance might substantially reduce insurance costs.

Developing data sources that would allow more systematic examination of the incidence of auto-insurance fraud, both across states and over time, would be valuable, particularly with respect to fraud perpetrated by organized rings. Many insurers suggested anecdotally that the growth of fraud in no-fault states contributed to its increased costs, but we lack the data to confirm or refute this explanation.

There are also substantial remaining gaps in our knowledge regarding no-fault and medical care. Two areas of particular priority are (1) better understanding how the insurance system and supply of physicians affect utilization of alternative medical providers and (2) identifying how different reimbursement systems for auto-related care may affect physicians' choice of treatment.[4]

## Likely Future Developments and Their Possible Implications

Three innovations—pay-as-you-drive auto insurance, autonomous-vehicle technology, and universal health care—may affect the relative advantages and disadvantages of no-fault and tort in compensating victims for automobile accidents. All three developments appear, as of this writing, reasonably likely to occur and would substantially affect automobile insurance and the relative desirability of no-fault automobile-insurance systems. We therefore offer these admittedly speculative preliminary thoughts.

### Pay-as-You-Drive Auto-Insurance Technology

Presently, auto insurance is usually sold on an all-you-can-eat basis. Drivers are required to purchase auto insurance that covers them, no matter how much or how little they drive.[5] Several insurers have introduced or plan to introduce pay-as-you-drive auto insurance priced by the number of miles that the driver actually drives (Edlin, 2003). Under most approaches, an electronic measurement unit installed in the car permits the insurance company to collect additional informa-

---

[4] A companion study (Heaton and Helland, 2009a) focusing on this second issue indicates that the more-generous reimbursements provided by no-fault cause physicians to change how they treat trauma cases. But it is less clear whether such effects are important in outpatient settings.

[5] While some policies offer discounts for low reported mileage, the discounts are relatively small, and the insurer has little means to monitor the driver's actual mileage.

tion about the vehicle. At the simplest level, this might include some means of verifying the number of miles actually driven. This would permit consumers to purchase insurance based on each marginal mile driven rather than simply pay a flat, fixed cost no matter how much or how little the car is driven.

Inexpensive Global Positioning System (GPS) tracking devices would permit consumers to purchase insurance priced based on when and where they are driving in addition to simply how many miles they drive. Accident rates vary widely by time of day and location. Consumers who drove at less crowded times and places could pay less. Rather than using the crude proxy of residence to estimate driving behavior, insurers could more carefully calibrate rates to the driver's actual driving times and locations.

At a more complex level, insurance could be priced based not just on where and when but on *how* a car is driven. Does the driver accelerate and brake suddenly or speed? Relatively inexpensive GPS technology could easily capture this data. A cautious driver who never speeds, accelerates gradually, and drives in low-accident times and places could purchase less-expensive insurance than another driver could.

These developments will permit insurance costs to more closely reflect expected accident costs and reduce the need for insurers to rely on comparatively crude proxies, such as residence, credit history, or kind of car, in order to try to predict driving behavior and likely claims. By being able to more accurately predict the expected accident cost of an individual driver, this technology will reduce cross-subsidization of worse drivers by better drivers.

After an accident, adjusters (and police) could use this technology to determine exactly what happened and to determine fault more precisely and inexpensively.[6]

---

[6]  Currently, some manufacturers use electronic data recorders in some automobiles, and some of those record accident data. But there is little standardization as to what these devices record or how accessible the data are (Erfle, 2008, p. 15). In October 2006, the National Highway Traffic Safety Administration (NHTSA) created new rules to standardize the information collected and the survivability of electronic data recorders. Litigation is ongoing as to the circumstances under which these data can be utilized after an accident.

How would the adoption of this approach affect the relative desirability of no-fault or tort insurance systems? We offer these admittedly speculative predictions: By reducing the cost of obtaining comparatively precise information after crashes, this technology might make the process of assigning fault for accidents less arbitrary and less expensive. Proponents of no-fault historically argued that identifying the party at fault was difficult and arbitrary.[7] Having readily available data following a crash on participants' relative speed and location would reduce this arbitrariness and make accurate determinations of fault more possible. Such data might reduce the costs of the tort system and BI insurance, to the extent that these costs reflect the administrative costs of determining fault.

**Autonomous-Vehicle Technology**
Automakers will increasingly offer technology that assists drivers in avoiding accidents. Such technology includes adaptive cruise control, driver monitoring systems, lane-departure warning systems, and autonomous parking technology. Honda presently sells a car in the United Kingdom that can steer itself using lane-keeping technology and accelerate or brake using adaptive cruise control. Volvo recently introduced technology to allow a car to brake itself when it senses an imminent collision with a car ahead of it (Kalra, Anderson, and Wachs, 2009). While these technologies will be introduced gradually, they (and their successors) have the potential to substantially change automobile transportation during the next 15 years.

How will these technologies affect automobile insurance? First, they will almost certainly reduce accident costs. Human error causes the vast majority of accidents today. By reducing the risk of human error, autonomous-vehicle technology can reduce accidents and, therefore, automobile-insurance costs under either PIP or BI. If accidents become infrequent enough, it is possible that the very need for specialized automobile insurance may disappear entirely. Injuries that result

---

[7]    But see Schwartz (2000), who argued that it is *easier* to ascertain fault in auto cases than in most other torts because traffic law is very detailed.

from the rare automobile accident might be covered by health insurance and homeowner's liability insurance.

Second, autonomous-vehicle technology may undermine the sense in which a driver must necessarily be at fault for an accident. Currently, the driver is considered primarily responsible for the control of a vehicle. Autonomous-vehicle technology will likely dilute the sense that drivers are directly and solely responsible. By shifting responsibility for the automobile from the human driver to the car or its manufacturer, these systems may undermine the conventional social attribution of blame for automobile accidents. This may lead to more litigation against car manufacturers and designers and less against car owners.

This technology may also change the distribution of accidents. Presently, minor accidents vastly outnumber the major ones. By reducing the importance of human error, autonomous-vehicle technology may be remarkably effective at virtually eliminating minor accidents. But it may be that the few accidents that remain are the result of software failures and could be catastrophic. This change in the cause and distribution of the seriousness of accidents would require substantial revision to the U.S. automobile-insurance system and would pose very different actuarial problems from those of the present distribution of a large number of relatively minor automobile accidents.

How will this development affect the relative desirability of no-fault and tort automobile-accident regimes? In the short run, it will depend on whether BI or PIP costs are more affected by the expected reduction in accidents. If this technology is most successful in reducing accidents in which a human being is legally at fault (and therefore subject to BI liability), it might reduce the comparative costs of tort.

On the other hand, this technology may greatly reduce or eliminate the category of accidents for which there is a driver to blame. If the only automobile accidents that remain are ones for which there is no at-fault driver, no-fault approaches may prove more politically attractive, particularly if the alternative is to otherwise leave a significant category of victims uncompensated.[8]

---

[8]   Product-liability suits against manufacturers *could* replace regular automobile-accident litigation, but this would be a dramatic change in the practice of auto-accident litigation.

Similarly, the technology may occasion a shift away from the conventional social norm of a driver as being solely responsible for the vehicle. This may make no-fault approaches more politically attractive.

## Universal Health Insurance

Many politicians have proposed some method of extending health coverage to all U.S. citizens. If legislation that created some form of universal health insurance were to pass, it could substantially change the economics of automobile insurance. In this monograph, we concluded that no-fault's decline in popularity is closely related to its expense, which, in turn, is driven primarily by medical costs. Many forms of universal health insurance would make it unnecessary for automobile insurance to cover medical costs, the most important and expensive component of BI and PIP coverage.[9]

Universal health insurance would probably make no-fault regimes more attractive because it would eliminate the largest source of cost inflation. Anecdotally, auto insurers have indicated that it is difficult to control rising medical costs paid through no-fault because the auto-insurance regulatory framework makes such controls more difficult than the essentially contractual framework permitted in health insurance, and because they do not have the expertise to run a first-party health-insurance operation.[10] Universal health insurance would simply eliminate this entire component of expenses if health insurance had priority (i.e., if claims were paid by health insurance prior to auto insurance).

---

[9]   PIP is currently usually prioritized over first-party medical coverage so that medical providers recover from PIP before billing other sources. Of course, it is possible that auto insurance as primary payer in auto accidents would be retained as some form of political compromise or means of reducing the costs of universal health care.

[10]   The social norms on pooling risks and cross-subsidization appear to be different for medical insurance and auto insurance. Most medical insurance is sold on a group basis, and efforts by the industry to have medical-insurance costs reflect differential risks of individual patients (by excluding patients with preexisting conditions, for example) have been met with political opposition. In contrast, there is no similar hostility to tailoring auto-insurance payments to individual risks (by experience rating, for example).

Studying the international experience with no-fault automobile insurance may provide some guidance on these issues. Israel, New Zealand, Saskatchewan, and Quebec, among others, have used no-fault automobile insurance, and all of them have different forms of health coverage. By studying their experience, we might learn better how the provision of universal health insurance might affect automobile insurance.

## Conclusion

No-fault automobile-insurance regimes were the culmination of decades of dissatisfaction with the use of the traditional tort system for compensating victims of automobile accidents. They offered the promise of quicker, fairer, less-contentious, and, it was hoped, less-expensive resolution of automobile-accident injuries. In this monograph, we look back to consider how these plans have fared. We conclude that no-fault claim costs generally proved higher than tort, largely as a result of substantially higher medical costs.

No-fault has therefore recently lost some of its appeal, and some insurers and consumer groups have stopped supporting it. Nonetheless, we think that it is premature to relegate no-fault to the dustbin of failed policy experiments. Allowing individual consumers in a state to choose limited tort appears, based on the Pennsylvania experience, a potentially promising way to control costs that bears further study. Similarly, many of the problems with tort that led to the adoption of no-fault may still exist. Finally, and most fundamentally, a state's choice of automobile-insurance regime is a political decision that is necessarily based on a range of equitable considerations. While consumer premium cost, the metric on which we primarily focused, is an important consideration, it is only one of many. Any decision to change automobile-insurance regimes should be based on a comprehensive evaluation of the advantages and disadvantages of the different systems.

# Required Insurance and Actual Insurance

In Table A.1, the liability minimums listed are called split limits. The first number listed is the amount of bodily injury for which the insured is covered for injuring one other person, the second number is the amount the insured is covered for in injuring more than one person, and the third number is the property damage covered.

**Table A.1**
**Liability Requirements**

| State | Liability Reqd[a] | Median BI Liability Coverage Bought[b] | Sample Size | PIP Reqd | PIP Min (in $k) | Limit on Recovery v. 3rd Parties? | UM Coverage Required? |
|---|---|---|---|---|---|---|---|
| Ala. | Yes, 20/40/10 | 100 | 516 | No | | No | No |
| Alaska | Yes, 50/100/25 | 300 | 83 | No | | No | No |
| Ariz. | Yes, 15/30/10 | 100 | 808 | No | | No | No |
| Ark. | Yes, 25/50/25 | 100 | 400 | No | | No | No |
| Calif. | Yes, 15/30/5[c] | 200 | 3,772 | No | | No | No |
| Colo. | Yes, 25/50/15 | 300 | 241 | No | | No | No |
| Conn. | Yes, 20/40/10 | 300 | 353 | No | | No | Yes |
| D.C. | Yes, 25/50/10 | 100 | 89 | No | | No | Yes |
| Del. | Yes, 15/30/10 | 300 | 143 | Yes | 15 | No | No |
| Fla. | No, 10/20/10 | 100 | 1,151 | Yes | 10 | Yes | No |
| Ga. | Yes, 25/50/25 | 100 | 1,126 | No | | No | No |
| Hawaii | Yes, 20/40/10 | 100 | 77 | Yes | 10 | Yes | No |
| Idaho | Yes, 25/50/15 | 300 | 163 | No | | No | No |
| Ill. | Yes, 20/40/15 | 300 | 1,469 | No | | No | Yes |
| Ind. | Yes, 25/50/10 | 300 | 551 | No | | No | No |
| Iowa | Yes, 20/40/15 | 300 | 163 | No | | No | No |

**Table A.1—Continued**

| State | Liability Reqd[a] | Median BI Liability Coverage Bought[b] | Sample Size | PIP Reqd | PIP Min (in $k) | Limit on Recovery v. 3rd Parties? | UM Coverage Required? |
|---|---|---|---|---|---|---|---|
| Kan. | Yes, 25/50/10 | 300 | 146 | Yes | 4.5 | Yes | Yes |
| Ky. | Yes, 25/50/10 | 100 | 314 | Yes | 10 | Yes | No |
| La. | Yes, 10/20/10 | 50 | 1,422 | No | | No | No |
| Maine[d] | Yes, 50/100/25 | 300 | 93 | No | | No | Yes |
| Mass. | Yes, 20/40/5 | 40 | 362 | Yes | 8 | Yes | Yes |
| Md. | Yes, 20/40/15 | 300 | 1,259 | Yes | 2.5 | No | Yes |
| Mich. | Yes, 20/40/10 | 300 | 205 | Yes | Unlimited | Yes | No |
| Minn. | Yes, 30/60/10 | 300 | 212 | Yes | 40 | Yes | Yes |
| Miss. | Yes, 25/50/25 | 50 | 285 | No | | No | No |
| Mo. | Yes, 25/50/10 | 100 | 811 | No | | No | Yes |
| Mont. | Yes, 25/50/10 | 100 | 85 | No | | No | No |
| N.C. | Yes, 30/60/25 | 100 | 1,439 | No | | No | No |
| N.D. | Yes, 25/50/25 | 300 | 9 | Yes | 30 | Yes | Yes |
| N.H. | No, 25/50/25 | 300 | 100 | No | | No | Yes |
| N.J. | Yes, 15/30/5 | 300 | 623 | Yes | 250 | Yes | Yes |
| N.M. | Yes, 25/50/10 | 100 | 261 | No | | No | No |

**Table A.1—Continued**

| State | Liability Reqd[a] | Median BI Liability Coverage Bought[b] | Sample Size | PIP Reqd | PIP Min (in $k) | Limit on Recovery v. 3rd Parties? | UM Coverage Required? |
|---|---|---|---|---|---|---|---|
| N.Y.[e] | Yes, 25/50/10 | 100 | 1,055 | Yes | 50 | Yes | Yes |
| Neb. | Yes, 25/50/25 | 300 | 260 | No | | No | No |
| Nev. | Yes, 15/30/10 | 60 | 391 | No | | No | No |
| Ohio | Yes, 12.5/25/7.5 | 300 | 1,441 | No | | No | No |
| Okla. | Yes, 25/50/25 | 50 | 695 | No | | No | No |
| Ore. | Yes, 25/50/10 | 300 | 606 | Yes | 10 | No | Yes |
| Pa. | Yes, 15/30/5 | 300 | 816 | Yes | 5 | Yes | No |
| R.I. | Yes, 25/50/25 | 200 | 131 | No | | No | Yes |
| S.C. | Yes, 25/50/25 | 50 | 1,044 | No | | No | Yes |
| S.D. | Yes, 25/50/25 | 300 | 48 | No | | No | Yes |
| Tenn. | Yes, 25/50/10 | 100 | 536 | No | | No | No |
| Texas | Yes, 25/50/25 | 50 | 3,256 | No | | No | No |
| Utah | Yes, 25/50/15 | 100 | 164 | Yes | 3 | Yes | No |
| Va. | Yes, 25/50/20 | 200 | 1,094 | Yes | 2 | No | Yes |
| Vt. | Yes, 25/50/10 | 300 | 44 | No | | No | Yes |
| W. Va. | Yes, 20/40/10 | 300 | 364 | No | | No | Yes |

**Table A.1—Continued**

| State | Liability Reqd[a] | Median BI Liability Coverage Bought[b] | Sample Size | PIP Reqd | PIP Min (in $k) | Limit on Recovery v. 3rd Parties? | UM Coverage Required? |
|---|---|---|---|---|---|---|---|
| Wash. | Yes, 25/50/10 | 300 | 632 | No | | No | No |
| Wis. | No, 25/50/10 | 300 | 408 | No | | No | Yes |
| Wyo. | Yes, 25/50/20 | 300 | 33 | No | | No | No |

[a] Liability minimums given In thousands of dollars.

[b] Maximum per accident in thousands of dollars. Based on Insurance Research Council's 2002 closed-claim data. Accordingly, it is the median insurance of insureds who filed claims. Because this sample may not be representative of the overall population of insureds, it should be interpreted with caution. The remainder of the data are taken from Insurance Information Institute (2009).

[c] Policy limits for drivers in the California Automobile Assigned Risk Plan are 10/20/3.

[d] In addition, policyholders must carry $1,000 for medical payments.

[e] In addition, policyholders must have 50/100 for wrongful-death coverage.

**Table A.2**
**Estimates and Standard Errors for Figure 5.12 in Chapter Five**

| Year | Tort | No-Fault | Mandatory Add-On | Optional Add-On |
|------|------|----------|------------------|-----------------|
| 1987 | 0.512 | 0.446 | 0.517 | 0.499 |
|      | (0.006) | (0.012) | (0.048) | (0.010) |
| 1992 | 0.517 | 0.491 | 0.522 | 0.515 |
|      | (0.005) | (0.015) | (0.033) | (0.007) |
| 1997 | 0.498 | 0.458 | 0.455 | 0.493 |
|      | (0.005) | (0.009) | (0.020) | (0.007) |
| 2002 | 0.459 | 0.446 | 0.466 | 0.423 |
|      | (0.007) | (0.010) | (0.021) | (0.009) |
| 2007 | 0.428 | 0.416 | 0.382 | 0.416 |
|      | (0.010) | (0.014) | (0.021) | (0.014) |

NOTE: The table reports the share of all payments by auto insurers that represented compensation for general damages. Bootstrapped standard errors using 1,000 replications are reported in parentheses.

# Bibliography

Abraham, Kenneth S., *The Liability Century: Insurance and Tort Law from the Progressive Era to 9/11*, Cambridge, Mass.: Harvard University Press, 2008.

Abrahamse, Allan, and Stephen J. Carroll, *The Effects of a Choice Auto Insurance Plan on Insurance Costs*, Santa Monica, Calif.: RAND Corporation, MG-540-ICJ, 1995. As of October 29, 2009:
http://www.rand.org/pubs/monograph_reports/MR540/

———, "The Effects of a Choice Automobile Insurance Plan on Insurance Costs and Compensation," *CPCU Journal*, Vol. 51, No. 1, Spring 1998, pp. 19–39.

All-Industry Research Advisory Council, *Compensation for Automobile Injuries in the United States*, Oak Brook, Ill., March 1989a.

———, *Claimant Satisfaction in Auto Accident Cases*, Oak Brook, Ill., June 1989b.

A. M. Best Company, *Best's Aggregates and Averages: Property/Casualty, United States and Canada*, Oldwick, N.J., 2008.

Ames, James B., "Law and Morals," *Harvard Law Review*, Vol. 22, 1908, pp. 97–113.

*Anderson v. Continental Ins. Co.*, 85 Wis. 2d 675, 271 N.W.2d 368, S.C. Wisc., October 31, 1978.

*Arambula v. Wells*, 72 Cal. App. 4th 1006, 85 Cal. Rptr. 2d 584, June 8, 1999.

Arnold, Morris S., "Accident, Mistake, and Rules of Liability in the Fourteenth-Century Law of Torts," *University of Pennsylvania Law Review*, Vol. 128, No. 2, December 1979, pp. 361–378.

Artís, Manuel, Mercedes Ayuso, and Montserrat Guillén, "Detection of Automobile Insurance Fraud with Discrete Choice Models and Misclassified Claims," *Journal of Risk and Insurance*, Vol. 69, No. 3, 2002, pp. 325–340.

Baker, John Hamilton, *An Introduction to English Legal History*, 2nd ed., London: Butterworths, 1979.

————, *An Introduction to English Legal History*, 3rd ed., London: Butterworths, 1990.

Baker, Tom, "Blood Money, New Money, and the Moral Economy of Tort Law in Action," *Law and Society Review*, Vol. 35, No. 2, 2001, pp. 275–320.

Ballantine, Arthur A., "A Compensation Plan for Railway Accident Claims," *Harvard Law Review*, Vol. 29, No. 7, May 1916, pp. 705–723.

BBC Research and Consulting, *Auto Insurance/Trauma System Study for State of Colorado*, Denver, Colo., February 18, 2008.

Bell, Judith, "Despite 103, Insurance Needs a Legislative Cure," *Los Angeles Times*, November 11, 1988, p. II-5.

Berte, Marjorie M., *Hit Me—I Need the Money! The Politics of Auto Insurance Reform*, San Francisco, Calif.: ICS Press, 1991.

BJS—*see* Bureau of Justice Statistics.

Blum, Walter J., and Harry Kalven, "Public Law Perspectives on a Private Law Problem: Auto Compensation Plans," *University of Chicago Law Review*, Vol. 31, No. 4, Summer 1964, pp. 641–723.

————, *Public Law Perspectives on a Private Law Problem: Auto Compensation Plans*, Boston, Mass.: Little, Brown, 1965.

————, "Ceilings, Costs, and Compulsion in Auto Compensation Legislation," *Utah Law Review*, Vol. 1973, No. 3, Fall 1973, pp. 341–382.

Bordoff, Jason E., and Pascal J. Noel, *Pay-as-You-Drive Auto Insurance: A Simple Way to Reduce Driving-Related Harms and Increase Equity*, Washington, D.C.: Brookings Institution, Hamilton Project discussion paper 2008-09, July 2008. As of December 1, 2009:
http://www.brookings.edu/~/media/Files/rc/papers/2008/07_payd_bordoffnoel/07_payd_bordoffnoel.pdf

*Boston Daily Globe*, October 29, 1955, p. 1, cols. 2–8.

*Brown v. Kendall*, 60 Mass. 292, October 1850.

Browne, Mark J., Ellen S. Pryor, and Bob Puelz, "The Effect of Bad-Faith Laws on First-Party Insurance Claims Decisions," *Journal of Legal Studies*, Vol. 33, 2004, pp. 355–390.

Bureau of Justice Statistics, *Civil Justice Survey of State Courts, 1996*, Ann Arbor, Mich.: Inter-University Consortium for Political and Social Research, National Archive of Criminal Justice Data, June 2004.

————, *Civil Justice Survey of State Courts, 2001*, Ann Arbor, Mich.: Inter-University Consortium for Political and Social Research, National Archive of Criminal Justice Data, November 2005.

————, *Civil Justice Survey of State Courts, 1992*, Ann Arbor, Mich.: Inter-University Consortium for Political and Social Research, National Archive of Criminal Justice Data, March 2006.

Burke, Thomas Frederick, *Lawyers, Lawsuits, and Legal Rights: The Battle over Litigation in American Society*, Berkeley, Calif.: University of California Press, 2002.

Butler, Richard J., and John D. Worrall, "Work Injury Compensation and the Duration of Nonwork Spells," *Economic Journal*, Vol. 95, No. 379, September 1985, pp. 714–724.

Calabresi, Guido, *The Costs of Accidents: A Legal and Economic Analysis*, New Haven, Conn.: Yale University Press, 1970.

————, *Ideals, Beliefs, Attitudes and the Law: Private Law Perspectives on a Public Law Problem*, Syracuse, N.Y.: Syracuse University Press, 1985.

Calabresi, Guido, and Jon T. Hirschoff, "Toward a Test for Strict Liability in Torts," *Yale Law Journal*, Vol. 81, No. 6, May 1972, pp. 1055–1085.

*Calfarm Ins. Co. v. Deukmejian*, 771 P.2d 1247, Cal. 1989.

California Insurance Code, Division 1, General Rules Governing Insurance, Part 2, The Business of Insurance, Chapter 1, General Regulations, Article 6.5, Unfair Practices, Section 790.03. As of December 1, 2009:
http://www.leginfo.ca.gov/cgi-bin/displaycode?section=ins&group=00001-01000&file=790-790.15

Carman, Ernest C., "Is a Motor Vehicle Accident Compensation Act Advisable?" *Minnesota Law Review*, Vol. 4, No. 1, December 1919, pp. 1–13.

Carroll, Stephen J., *Effects of an Auto-Choice Automobile Insurance Plan on Costs and Premiums*, Santa Monica, Calif.: RAND Corporation, CT-141-1, 1997. As of October 29, 2009:
http://www.rand.org/pubs/testimonies/CT141-1/

Carroll, Stephen J., and Allan Abrahamse, *The Effects of a Choice Automobile Insurance Plan on Insurance Costs and Compensation: An Updated Analysis*, Santa Monica, Calif.: RAND Corporation, MR-970-ICJ, 1998. As of October 29, 2009:
http://www.rand.org/pubs/monograph_reports/MR970/

Carroll, Stephen J., Allan Abrahamse, and Mary E. Vaiana, *The Costs of Excess Medical Claims for Automobile Personal Injuries*, Santa Monica, Calif.: RAND Corporation, DB-139-ICJ, 1995. As of October 29, 2009:
http://www.rand.org/pubs/documented_briefings/DB139/

Carroll, Stephen J., James S. Kakalik, Nicholas M. Pace, and John L. Adams, *No-Fault Approaches to Compensating People Injured in Automobile Accidents*, Santa Monica, Calif.: RAND Corporation, R-4019-ICJ, 1991. As of October 29, 2009:
http://www.rand.org/pubs/reports/R4019/

Centers for Medicare and Medicaid Services, "National Health Expenditure Data: Overview," undated. As of December 7, 2009:
http://www.cms.hhs.gov/NationalHealthExpendData/

Clark, Roger S., and Gerald E. Waterson, "'No-Fault' in Delaware," *Rutgers Camden Law Journal*, Vol. 6, No. 2, 1974, pp. 225–264.

CMS—*see* Centers for Medicare and Medicaid Services.

Cohen, Alma, and Rajeev Dehejia, "The Effect of Automobile Insurance and Accident Liability Laws on Traffic Fatalities," *Journal of Law and Economics*, Vol. 47, No. 2, October 2004, pp. 357–393.

Cole, Cassandra R., Kevin Eastman, David A. MacPherson, Patrick F. Maroney, and Kathleen A. McCullough, *The Impact of No-Fault Legislation on Automobile Insurance Premiums*, working paper, February 2008.

Coleman, Jules L., *Risks and Wrongs*, Cambridge, Mass.: Cambridge University Press, 1992.

Committee to Study Compensation for Automobile Accidents, Columbia University Council for Research in the Social Sciences, *Report, by the Committee to Study Compensation for Automobile Accidents: To the Columbia University Council for Research in the Social Sciences*, Philadelphia, Pa.: Press of International Print, 1932.

Conard, Alfred Fletcher, *Automobile Accident Costs and Payments: Studies in the Economics of Injury Reparation*, Ann Arbor, Mich.: University of Michigan Press, 1964.

Connecticut General Statutes, Title 38a, Insurance, Chapter 700, Property and Casualty Insurance, Section 38a-321, Liability of Insurer Under Liability Policy. As of December 1, 2009:
http://www.cga.ct.gov/2009/pub/chap700.htm#Sec38a-321.htm

Craddock, Ashley, and Mordecai Lawrence, "Swoop-and-Squats," *Mother Jones Magazine*, September–October 1993, pp. 16–30.

Crocker, Keith J., and John Morgan, "Is Honesty the Best Policy? Curtailing Insurance Fraud Through Optimal Incentive Contracts," *Journal of Political Economy*, Vol. 106, No. 2, April 1998, pp. 355–375.

Crocker, Keith J., and Sharon Tennyson, "Insurance Fraud and Optimal Claims Settlement Strategies," *Journal of Law and Economics*, Vol. 45, No. 2, October 2002, pp. 469–507.

Cummins, J. David, ed., *Deregulating Property-Liability Insurance: Restoring Competition and Increasing Market Efficiency*, Washington, D.C.: AEI-Brookings Joint Center for Regulatory Studies, 2002.

Cummins, J. David, Richard D. Phillips, and Mary A. Weiss, "The Incentive Effects of No-Fault Automobile Insurance," *Journal of Law and Economics*, Vol. 44, No. 2, October 2001, pp. 427–464.

Cummins, J. David, and Sharon Tennyson, "Controlling Automobile Insurance Costs," *Journal of Economic Perspectives*, Vol. 6, No. 2, Spring 1992, pp. 95–115.

Cummins, J. David, and Mary A. Weiss, "The Stochastic Dominance of No-Fault Automobile Insurance," *Journal of Risk and Insurance*, Vol. 60, No. 2, June 1993, pp. 230–264.

Davies, Jack, "A No-Fault History," *William Mitchell Law Review*, Vol. 24, No. 4, 1998, pp. 839–848.

Delaware Code, Title 18, Insurance Code, Chapter 23, Unfair Practices in the Insurance Business, Section 2304, Unfair Methods of Competition and Unfair or Deceptive Acts or Practices Defined. As of December 1, 2009: http://delcode.delaware.gov/title18/c023/index.shtml

Derrig, Richard A., "Insurance Fraud," *Journal of Risk and Insurance*, Vol. 69, No. 3, September 2002, pp. 271–287.

Derrig, Richard A., Maria Segui-Gomez, Ali Abtahi, and Ling-Ling Liu, "The Effect of Population Safety Belt Usage Rates on Motor Vehicle–Related Fatalities," *Accident Analysis and Prevention*, Vol. 34, No. 1, 2002, pp. 101–110.

Derrig, Richard A., Herbert I. Weisberg, and Xiu Chen, "Behavioral Factors and Lotteries Under No-Fault with a Monetary Threshold: A Study of Massachusetts Automobile Claims," *Journal of Risk and Insurance*, Vol. 61, No. 2, June 1994, pp. 245–275.

Devlin, Rose Anne, "Liability Versus No-Fault Automobile Insurance Regimes: An Analysis of the Experience in Quebec," in Georges Dionne, ed., *Contributions to Insurance Economics*, Boston, Mass.: Kluwer Academic Publishers, 1992, pp. 499–520.

Dewees, Donald N., David Duff, and M. J. Trebilcock, *Exploring the Domain of Accident Law: Taking the Facts Seriously*, New York and Oxford: Oxford University Press, 1996.

Dorsett, J. Dewey, *Report to the Annual Meeting of the Association for Casualty and Surety Companies*, New York: Association of Casualty and Surety Companies, 1950.

DOT—*see* U.S. Department of Transportation.

Dowling, Noel T., "Compensation for Automobile Compensation: A Symposium," *Columbia Law Review*, Vol. 32, No. 5, 1932, pp. 785–824.

"The Drama with a Case of 100 Million," *Trial*, Vol. 4, No. 2, 1968, p. 26.

Edlin, Aaron S., "Per-Mile Premiums for Auto Insurance," in Richard Arnott, Bruce Greenwald, Ravi Kanbur, and Barry Nalebuff, eds., *Economics for an Imperfect World: Essays in Honor of Joseph E. Stiglitz*, Cambridge, Mass.: MIT Press, 2003, pp. 53–82.

Edward VII Statutes, Title 6, 1906.

Ehrenzweig, Albert Armin, *"Full Aid" Insurance for the Traffic Victim*, Berkeley, Calif.: University of California Press, 1954.

Elsbree, Wayland H., and Harold Cooper Roberts, "Compulsory Insurance Against Motor Vehicle Accidents," *University of Pennsylvania Law Review and American Law Register*, Vol. 76, No. 6, April 1928, pp. 690–703.

Emergency Medical Treatment and Active Labor Act—*see* Public Law 99-272.

*Employees' Benefit Ass'n v. Grissett*, 732 So. 2d 968, S.C. Ala., September 11, 1998.

Enzer, Selwyn, *Some Impacts of No-Fault Automobile Insurance: A Technology Assessment*, Menlo Park, Calif.: Institute for the Future, 1974.

Epstein, Richard A., "Automobile No-Fault Plans: A Second Look at First Principles," *Creighton Law Review*, Vol. 13, 1980, pp. 769–794.

Erfle, Nancy M., "Learning to Live with Electronic Data Recorders," *The Brief*, Vol. 38, Fall 2008.

Fishback, Price Van Meter, and Shawn Everett Kantor, *A Prelude to the Welfare State: The Origins of Workers' Compensation*, Chicago, Ill.: University of Chicago Press, 2000.

Fleming, John G., "The Collateral Source Rule and Loss Allocation in Tort Law," *California Law Review*, Vol. 54, No. 4, October 1966, pp. 1478–1549.

*Fletcher v. Western National Life Ins. Co.*, 10 Cal. App. 3d 376, 89 Cal. Rptr. 78, Ct. App., August 7, 1970.

Florida Statutes, Title XXIII, Motor Vehicles, Chapter 324, Financial Responsibility, Section 324.031, Manner of Proving Financial Responsibility. As of November 24, 2009:
http://www.leg.state.fl.us/STATUTES/index.cfm?App_mode=Display_Statute&Search_String=&URL=Ch0324/SEC031.HTM&Title=->2009->Ch0324->Section%20031#0324.031

———, Title XXXVII, Insurance, Chapter 624, Insurance Code: Administration and General Provisions, Part I, Scope of Code, Section 624.155, Civil Remedy. As of December 1, 2009:
http://www.leg.state.fl.us/STATUTES/index.cfm?App_mode=Display_Statute&Search_String=&URL=Ch0624/SEC155.HTM&Title=-%3E2009-%3ECh0624-%3ESection%20155#0624.155

————, Title XXXVII, Insurance, Chapter 627, Insurance Rates and Contracts, Section 627.737, Tort Exemption, Limitation on Right to Damages, Punitive Damages. As of January 5, 2010:
http://www.leg.state.fl.us/STATUTES/index.cfm?App_mode=Display_Statute&Search_String=&URL=Ch0627/Sec737.HTM

Franklin, Marc A., Robert L. Rabin, and Michael D. Green, *Tort Law and Alternatives: Cases and Materials*, 8th ed., New York: Foundation Press, 2006.

French, Patterson H., *The Automobile Compensation Plan: A Solution for Some Problems of Court Congestion and Accident Litigation in New York State*, New York: Columbia University Press, 1933.

*Frost v. Porter Leasing Corp.*, 386 Mass. 425; 436 N.E.2d 387, Supreme Judicial Court of Massachusetts, June 3, 1982.

Galanter, Marc, "Real World Torts: An Antidote to Anecdote," *Maryland Law Review*, Vol. 55, 1996, pp. 1093–1160.

Gawande, Atul, "The Cost Conundrum: What a Texas Town Can Teach Us About Health Care," *New Yorker*, June 1, 2009, pp. 36–44. As of December 1, 2009:
http://www.newyorker.com/reporting/2009/06/01/090601fa_fact_gawande

Georgia Code, Title 33, Insurance, Chapter 4, Actions Against Insurance Companies, Section 33-4-6, Liability of Insurer for Damages and Attorney's Fees, Notice to Commissioner of Insurance and Consumers' Insurance Advocate.

————, Title 33, Insurance, Chapter 6, Unfair Trade Practices, Article 2, Unfair Claims Settlement Practices, Section 33-6-34, Unfair Claims Settlement Practices.

German Statutes, Employers' Liability Law of 1871.

————, Accident Insurance Bill of 1884.

Gilles, Stephen G., "Inevitable Accident in Classical English Tort Law," *Emory Law Journal*, Vol. 43, No. 2, 1994, pp. 575–646.

Goldberg, John C. P., "Twentieth-Century Tort Theory Symposium: The New Negligence," *Georgetown Law Journal*, Vol. 91, March 2003, pp. 513–584.

Green, Leon, *Traffic Victims: Tort Law and Insurance*, Evanston, Ill.: Northwestern University Press, 1958.

Gregory, Charles O., "Trespass to Negligence to Absolute Liability," *Virginia Law Review*, Vol. 37, No. 3, April 1951, pp. 359–398.

*Gruenberg v. Aetna Ins. Co.*, 9 Cal. 3d 566, 510 P.2d 1032, 108 Cal. Rptr. 480, S. Ct. Calif., June 11, 1973.

Haller, John S. Jr., "Industrial Accidents—Worker Compensation Laws and the Medical Response," *Western Journal of Medicine*, Vol. 148, No. 3, March 1988, pp. 341–348.

Handley, Fletcher D. Jr., testimony before the U.S. Senate Committee on Commerce, Science, and Transportation, June 9, 1999.

Harrington, Scott E., "State Decisions to Limit Tort Liability: An Empirical Analysis of No-Fault Automobile Insurance Laws," *Journal of Risk and Insurance*, Vol. 61, No. 2, June 1994, pp. 276–294.

Hawaii Statutes, Vol. 9, Chapter 421, Section 13-102, Unfair Methods of Competition, Unfair or Deceptive Acts or Practices. As of December 1, 2009: http://www.capitol.hawaii.gov/hrscurrent/Vol09_Ch0431-0435E/HRS0431/ HRS_0431-0013-0102.htm

Hawken, Angela, Stephen J. Carroll, and Allan Abrahamse, *The Effects of Third-Party, Bad Faith Doctrine on Automobile Insurance Costs and Compensation*, Santa Monica, Calif.: RAND Corporation, MR-1199-ICJ, 2001. As of October 30, 2009: http://www.rand.org/pubs/monograph_reports/MR1199/

Heaton, Paul, and Eric Helland, *Does Treatment Respond to Reimbursement Rates? Evidence from Trauma Care*, RAND Corporation, WR-648-ICJ, 2009a. As of October 29, 2009: http://www.rand.org/pubs/working_papers/WR648/

———, *No-Fault Insurance and Automobile Accidents*, Santa Monica, Calif.: RAND Corporation, WR-551-ICJ, 2009b. As of October 29, 2009: http://www.rand.org/pubs/working_papers/WR551/

Heckman, Candace, "Does Insurance Company 'Low-Ball' Pain and Suffering?" *Seattle Post-Intelligencer*, May 15, 2003. As of December 1, 2009: http://www.seattlepi.com/local/122105_colossus15xx.html

Henle, John, *Rehabilitation of Auto Accident Victims: Prepared for the Dept. of Transportation Automobile Insurance and Compensation Study*, Washington, D.C., 1970.

Hensler, Deborah R., M. Susan Marquis, Allan Abrahamse, Sandra H. Berry, Patricia A. Ebener, Elizabeth Lewis, Edgar Lind, Robert MacCoun, Willard G. Manning, Jeannette Rogowski, and Mary E. Vaiana, *Compensation for Accidental Injuries in the United States*, Santa Monica, Calif.: RAND Corporation, R-3999-HHS/ICJ, 1991. As of October 29, 2009: http://www.rand.org/pubs/reports/R3999/

Hensley, Roy J., *Competition, Regulation, and the Public Interest in Nonlife Insurance*, Berkeley, Calif.: University of California Press, 1962.

Hoffman, Jan, "Life on Wheels: New No-Fault Insurance Effort Emerges in Capitol," *Los Angeles Times*, February 9, 1989, pp. IX–3. As of December 1, 2009: http://articles.latimes.com/1989-02-09/news/li-3127_1_no-fault-insurance

Holmes, Oliver Wendell Jr., *The Common Law*, Boston, Mass.: Little, Brown, and Company, 1881.

Horwitz, Morton J., *The Transformation of American Law, 1780–1860*, Cambridge, Mass.: Harvard University Press, 1977.

Houser, Douglas G., Ronald J. Clark, and Linda M. Bolduan, "Good Faith as a Matter of Law—An Update on the Insurance Company's 'Right to Be Wrong,'" *Tort Trial and Insurance Practice Law Journal*, Vol. 27, No. 665, 2003–2004, pp. 1045–1092.

H.R. 1475—*see* U.S. House of Representatives (1999).

Hunter, Robert, testimony before U.S. Congress Joint Economic Committee, March 19, 1997.

—————, director of insurance, Consumer Federation of America, interview with the author, May 21, 2008.

Illinois Compiled Statutes, Chapter 215, Insurance, 5, Illinois Insurance Code, Article IX, Provisions Applicable to All Companies, Section 155, Attorney Fees. As of December 1, 2009:
http://www.ilga.gov/legislation/ilcs/ilcs5.asp?ActID=1249&ChapAct=215%26nbsp;ILCS%26nbsp;5/&ChapterID=22&ChapterName=INSURANCE&ActName=Illinois+Insurance+Code.

Insurance Information Institute, "Auto Insurance," undated Web page. As of October 30, 2009:
http://www.iii.org/media/facts/statsbyissue/auto/

—————, *Insurance Facts*, New York, 1976.

—————, *No-Fault Automobile Insurance*, New York, 2007.

—————, *Insurance Fact Book*, New York, 2009.

Insurance Research Council, *Auto Injury Insurance Claims: Countrywide Patterns in Treatment, Cost, and Compensation*, Malvern, Pa., 1993.

—————, *Auto Injuries: Claiming Behavior and Its Impact on Insurance Costs*, Oak Brook, Ill., 1994a.

—————, *Paying for Auto Injuries: A Consumer Panel Survey of Auto Accident Victims*, Oak Brook, Ill., May 1994b.

—————, *Injuries in Auto Accidents: An Analysis of Auto Insurance Claims*, Malvern, Pa., June 1999a.

—————, *Paying for Auto Injuries: A Consumer Panel Survey of Auto Accident Victims*, Malvern, Pa., September 1999b.

—————, *Auto Injury Insurance Claims: Countrywide Patterns in Treatment, Cost, and Compensation*, 2004 ed., Malvern, Pa., 2003.

—————, *Paying for Auto Injuries: A Consumer Panel Survey of Auto Accident Victims*, Malvern, Pa., August 2004.

————, *Uninsured Motorists*, Malvern, Pa., 2006.

————, *Alternative Medical Treatment in Auto Injury Insurance Claims*, Malvern, Pa., September 2007.

————, *Trends in Auto Injury Claims*, Malvern, Pa., 2008a.

————, *Auto Injury Insurance Claims: Countrywide Patterns in Treatment, Cost, and Compensation*, 2008 ed., Malvern, Pa., January 2008b.

Iowa Code, Title XIII, Commerce, Subtitle 1, Insurance and Related Regulation, Chapter 516, Liability Policies, Unsatisfied Judgments, 516.1, Inurement of Policy. As of December 1, 2009:
http://coolice.legis.state.ia.us/Cool-ICE/default.asp?category=billinfo&service=IowaCode&ga=83

IRC—*see* Insurance Research Council.

*Ives v. South B. R. Co.*, 201 N.Y. 271; 94 N.E. 431, Ct. App. N.Y., March 24, 1911.

James, Fleming, and Stuart C. Law, "Compensation for Auto Accident Victims: A Story of Too Little and Too Late," *Connecticut Bar Journal*, Vol. 26, 1952, pp. 70–81.

Johnson, Joseph E., George B. Flanigan, and Daniel T. Winkler, "Cost Implications of No-Fault Automobile Insurance," *Journal of Risk and Insurance*, Vol. 59, No. 1, March 1992, pp. 116–123.

Jones, Thomas C., insurance commissioner, Michigan, "No Fault Automobile Insurance in Michigan: A Preliminary Study," in Alan I. Widiss, ed., *No Fault Automobile Insurance in Action: The Experiences in Massachusetts, Florida, Delaware and Michigan*, Dobbs Ferry, N.Y.: Oceana Publications, 1977, pp. 379–381.

Kachalia, Allen, Michelle M. Mello, Troyen A. Brennan, and David M. Studdert, "Beyond Negligence: Avoidability and Medical Injury Compensation," *Social Science and Medicine*, Vol. 66, No. 2, January 2008, pp. 387–402. As of December 1, 2009:
http://dx.doi.org/10.1016/j.socscimed.2007.08.020

Kafka, Franz, *The Trial*, New York: Knopf, 1956.

Kalra, Nidhi, James Anderson, and Martin Wachs, *Liability and Regulation of Autonomous Vehicle Technologies*, Berkeley, Calif.: California PATH Program, Institute of Transportation Studies, University of California at Berkeley, UCB-ITS-PRR-2009-28, April 2009.

Keeton, Robert E., and Jeffrey O'Connell, *Basic Protection for the Traffic Victim: A Blueprint for Reforming Automobile Insurance*, Toronto, Ont.: Little, Brown, 1965.

Keeton, William R., and Evan Kwerel, "Externalities in Automobile Insurance and the Underinsured Driver Problem," *Journal of Law and Economics*, Vol. 27, No. 1, April 1984, pp. 149–180.

King, Josephine Y., "The Insurance Industry and Compensation Plans," *New York University Law Review*, Vol. 43, No. 6, 1968, pp. 1137–1170.

Kinzler, Peter, *Auto Insurance Reform Options: How to Change State Tort and No-Fault Laws to Reduce Premiums and Increase Consumer Choice*, Indianapolis, Ind.: National Association of Mutual Insurance Companies, public policy paper, August 2006.

Knepper, William E., "Law, Insurance and the Automobile Accident Victim: A Defense of the Present Legal System," *Journal of Insurance*, Vol. 29, No. 2, June 1962, pp. 159–167.

Kochanowski, Paul S., and Madelyn V. Young, "Deterrent Aspects of No-Fault Automobile Insurance: Some Empirical Findings," *Journal of Risk and Insurance*, Vol. 52, No. 2, June 1985, pp. 269–288.

Kozyris, P. John, "No-Fault Automobile Insurance and the Conflict of Laws: Cutting the Gordian Knot Home-Style," *Duke Law Journal*, Vol. 1972, No. 2, June 1972, pp. 331–406.

Kramer, Donald W., "Fallacies of a Compensation Plan for Automobile Accident Litigation," *Insurance Counsel Journal*, Vol. 26, No. 3, July 1959, pp. 420–424.

Kretzmer, David, "No-Fault Comes to Israel: The Compensation for Victims of Road Accidents Law 1975," *Israel Law Review*, Vol. 11, Vol. 2, 1976, pp. 288–311.

Kunreuther, Howard, "The Economics of Protection Against Low Probability Events," in Gerardo R. Ungson and Daniel N. Braunstein, eds., *Decision Making: An Interdisciplinary Inquiry*, Boston, Mass.: Kent Publishing Company, 1982, pp. 195–209.

Landes, Elisabeth M., "Insurance, Liability, and Accidents: A Theoretical and Empirical Investigation of the Effect of No-Fault Accidents," *Journal of Law and Economics*, Vol. 25, No. 1, April 1982, pp. 49–65.

Landes, William M., and Richard A. Posner, *The Economic Structure of Tort Law*, Cambridge, Mass.: Harvard University Press, 1987.

Landis, James, "Book Review," *Harvard Law Review*, Vol. 45, No. 8, June 1932, pp. 1428–1430.

Lascher, Edward L., *The Politics of Automobile Insurance Reform: Ideas, Institutions, and Public Policy in North America*, Washington, D.C.: Georgetown University Press, 1999.

Lascher, Edward L., and Michael R. Powers, eds., *The Economics and Politics of Choice No-Fault Insurance*, Boston, Mass.: Kluwer Academic Publishers, 2001.

Liao, Yu-Ping, and Michelle J. White, "No-Fault for Motor Vehicles: An Economic Analysis," *American Law and Economics Review*, Vol. 4, No. 2, 2002, pp. 258–294.

Liberto, Jennifer, "Insurance: No-Fault's End? A Quiet, Big Deal," *St. Petersburg Times*, February 18, 2007. As of November 25, 2009:
http://www.sptimes.com/2007/02/18/Opinion/INSURANCE__No_fault_s.shtml

Liebman, Jeffrey B., and Richard Zeckhauser, *Simple Human, Complex Insurance, Subtle Subsidies*, Cambridge, Mass.: National Bureau of Economic Research, Working Paper 14330, September 2008. As of November 25, 2009:
http://www.nber.org/papers/w14330

Lilly, Austin J., "Compensation for Automobile Accidents: A Symposium—Criticism of the Proposed Solution," *Columbia Law Review*, Vol. 32, 1932, pp. 803–812.

Loughran, David S., *The Effect of No-Fault Automobile Insurance on Driver Behavior and Automobile Accidents in the United States*, Santa Monica, Calif.: RAND Corporation, MR-1384-ICJ, 2001. As of October 29, 2009:
http://www.rand.org/pubs/monograph_reports/MR1384/

———, "Deterring Fraud: The Role of General Damage Awards in Automobile Insurance Settlements," *Journal of Risk and Insurance*, Vol. 72, No. 4, 2005, pp. 551–575.

*MacPherson v. Buick Motor Co.*, 217 N.Y. 382, 111 N.E. 1050, Ct. App. N.Y., March 14, 1916.

Madden, Emmett, attorney, interview with the author, Philadelphia, Pa., June 19, 2008.

Magnuson-Moss Warranty Act—*see* Public Law 93-637.

Malone, Wex S., "Ruminations on the Role of Fault in the History of the Common Law of Torts," *Louisiana Law Review*, Vol. 31, No. 1, 1970, pp. 1–44.

"Mandatory Auto Insurance Does Not Reduce Number of Uninsured Drivers, Says Insurer Trade Group," *Insurance Journal*, July 25, 2004. As of November 24, 2009:
http://www.insurancejournal.com/news/national/2004/07/25/44371.htm

Marx, Robert S., "Compulsory Compensation Insurance," *Columbia Law Review*, Vol. 25, No. 2, February 1925, pp. 164–193.

Mashaw, Jerry L., and David L. Harfst, *The Struggle for Auto Safety*, Cambridge, Mass.: Harvard University Press, September 1990.

Massachusetts General Laws, Part I, Administration of the Government, Title XIV, Public Ways and Works, Chapter 90, Motor Vehicles and Aircraft, Sections 34A–34R, Compulsory Motor Vehicle Liability Insurance.

————, Part I, Administration of the Government, Title XV, Regulation of Trade, Chapter 93A, Regulation of Business Practices for Consumers Protection, Section 9, Civil Actions and Remedies, Class Action, Demand for Relief, Damages, Costs, Exhausting Administrative Remedies. As of December 1, 2009: http://www.mass.gov/legis/laws/mgl/93a-9.htm

Mayerson, Marc S., "'First Party' Insurance Bad Faith Claims: Mooring Procedure to Substance," *Tort Trial and Insurance Practice Law Journal*, Vol. 38, No. 3, Spring 2003, pp. 861–886.

McEwin, R. Ian, "No-Fault and Road Accidents: Some Australasian Evidence," *International Review of Law and Economics*, Vol. 9, No. 1, June 1989, pp. 13–24.

Mello, Michelle M., and Troyen A. Brennan, "Deterrence of Medical Errors: Theory and Evidence for Malpractice Reform," *Texas Law Review*, Vol. 80, 2002, pp. 1595–1638.

Meyer, Bruce D., W. Kip Viscusi, and David L. Durbin, "Workers' Compensation and Injury Duration: Evidence from a Natural Experiment," *American Economic Review*, Vol. 85, No. 3, June 1995, pp. 332–340.

Michigan Compiled Laws, Chapter 500, Insurance Code of 1956, Act 218 of 1956, The Insurance Code of 1956 (Excerpt), Chapter 31, Motor Vehicle Personal and Property Protection, Section 500.3135, Tort Liability for Noneconomic Loss, Action for Damages Pursuant to Subsection (1), Abolition of Tort Liability, Exceptions, Action for Damages Pursuant to Subsection (3)(d), Commencement of Action, Removal, Costs, Decision as Res Judicata, "Serious Impairment of Body Function" Defined. As of January 5, 2010: http://www.legislature.mi.gov/(S(c1j4zofgnwb2dsjx3um0ahqi))/mileg.aspx?page=sh ortlinkdisplay&docname=mcl-500-3135

Missouri Revised Statutes, Title XXIV, Business and Financial Institutions, Chapter 375, Provisions Applicable to All Insurance Companies, Section 375.420, Vexatious Refusal to Pay Claim, Damages for, Exception. As of December 1, 2009: http://www.moga.mo.gov/statutes/C300-399/3750000420.HTM

Montana Code, Title 33, Insurance and Insurance Companies, Chapter 18, Unfair Trade Practices, Part 2, Insurer's Relations with Insured and Claimant, Section 33-18-242, Independent Cause of Action, Burden of Proof. As of December 1, 2009: http://data.opi.state.mt.us/bills/mca/33/18/33-18-242.htm

Morris, Clarence, and James C. N. Paul, "The Financial Impact of Automobile Accidents," *University of Pennsylvania Law Review*, Vol. 110, No. 7, May 1962, pp. 913–933.

NACJD—*see* National Archive of Criminal Justice Data.

Nader, Ralph, testimony before the U.S. Senate Committee on Commerce, Science, and Transportation, June 9, 1999.

National Archive of Criminal Justice Data, *State Court Statistics, 1985–2001*, November 11, 2005. As of January 5, 2010:
http://dx.doi.org/10.3886/ICPSR09266

———, *State Court Statistics, 2002*, January 18, 2006. As of January 5, 2010:
http://dx.doi.org/10.3886/ICPSR03990

———, *State Court Statistics, 2003*, November 14, 2007a. As of January 5, 2010:
http://dx.doi.org/10.3886/ICPSR20280

———, *State Court Statistics, 2004*, November 14, 2007b. As of January 5, 2010:
http://dx.doi.org/10.3886/ICPSR20281

National Center for State Courts, State Court Statistics Series, 1985–2004. As of December 14, 2009:
http://www.icpsr.org/cocoon/NACJD/SERIES/00080.xml

National Highway Traffic Safety Administration, *Annual Assessment of Motor Vehicle Crashes*, Washington, D.C., 2008.

New Hampshire Statutes, Title XXI, Motor Vehicles, Chapter 264, Accidents and Financial Responsibility, Section 264:20, Amount of Proof of Financial Responsibility. As of November 24, 2009:
http://www.gencourt.state.nh.us/rsa/html/XXI/264/264-20.htm

New Jersey Statutes, Title 39, Motor Vehicles and Traffic Regulation, Section 6A-8, Tort Exemption, Limitation on the Right to Noneconomic Loss.

*New York Central Railroad v. White*, 243 U.A. 188, 1916.

New York Statutes, ISC (Insurance) Article 51, Comprehensive Motor Vehicle Insurance Reparations, Section 5102, Definitions.

NHTSA—*see* National Highway Traffic Safety Administration.

Noce, Gerard T., testimony before the U.S. Senate Committee on Commerce, Science, and Transportation, June 9, 1999.

Nordman, Eric, "The History of No-Fault Auto Insurance," *Journal of Insurance Regulation*, Vol. 16, No. 4, 1998, pp. 457–466.

Norman, Leslie George, *Road Traffic Accidents: Epidemiology, Control, and Prevention*, Geneva, Switzerland: World Health Organization, Public Health Papers, No. 12, 1962.

O'Connell, Jeffrey, *Ending Insult to Injury: No-Fault Insurance for Products and Services*, Urbana, Ill.: University of Illinois Press, 1975.

———, "Allowing Motorists a Choice to Be Legally Uninsured by Surrendering Tort Claims for Noneconomic Loss (with Some Further Thoughts on Choices Between PIP and Tort Coverage)," *Connecticut Insurance Law Journal*, Vol. 1, Spring 1995, pp. 33–66.

———, interview with the author, June 24, 2008.

O'Connell, Jeffrey, Stephen J. Carroll, Michael J. Horowitz, and Allan F. Abrahamse, "Consumer Choice in the Auto Insurance Market," *Maryland Law Review*, Vol. 52, No. 4, 1993, pp. 1016–1062. Reprint RP-254 (1994), as of December 1, 2009:
http://www.rand.org/pubs/reprints/RP254/

O'Connell, Jeffrey, Stephen J. Carroll, Michael J. Horowitz, Allan F. Abrahamse, Lewis Jamison, and Paul F. Jamieson, "The Comparative Costs of Allowing Consumer Choice for Auto Insurance in All Fifty States," *Maryland Law Review*, Vol. 55, No. 1, 1996, pp. 160–222. Reprint RP-518 (1996), as of December 1, 2009:
http://www.rand.org/pubs/reprints/RP518/

O'Connell, Jeffrey, Stephen J. Carroll, Michael J. Horowitz, Allan F. Abrahamse, and Daniel Kaiser, "The Costs of Consumer Choice for Auto Insurance in States Without No-Fault Insurance," *Maryland Law Review*, Vol. 54, No. 2, 1995, pp. 281–351. Reprint RP-442 (1995), as of December 1, 2009:
http://www.rand.org/pubs/reprints/RP442/

O'Connell, Jeffrey, and Robert H. Joost, "Giving Motorists a Choice Between Fault and No-Fault Insurance," *Virginia Law Review*, Vol. 72, No. 1, February 1986, pp. 61–89.

O'Connell, Jeffrey, and John Linehan, "Neo No-Fault Early Offers: A Workable Compromise Between First and Third-Party Insurance," *Gonzaga Law Review*, Vol. 41, No. 1, 2005–2006, pp. 103–150.

Oliphant, Ken, "Landmarks of No-Fault in the Common Law," in Willem H. van Boom and Michael Faure, eds., *Shifts in Compensation Between Private and Public Systems*, New York: Springer-Verlag, 2007, pp. 43–86.

Ontario Legislative Assembly, *Final Report, Select Committee to Examine into and to Report on All Matters Relating to Persons Who Suffer Financial Loss or Injury as a Result of Motor Vehicle Accidents*, Toronto, Ont., March 1963.

Outreville, Jean-Francois, "The Impact of the Government No-Fault Plan for Automobile Insurance in the Province of Quebec," *Journal of Risk and Insurance*, Vol. 51, No. 2, June 1984, pp. 320–335.

Peck, Robert S., president, Center for Constitutional Litigation, "Retrospective on No-Fault," email to the author, Washington, D.C., April 30, 2009.

Pennsylvania Consolidated Statutes, Title 75, Vehicles, Part II, Title, Registration and Licensing, Chapter 16, Commercial Drivers, Section 1602, Purpose and Construction of Chapter.

Phillips, Jerry J., and Stephen Chippendale, *Who Pays for Car Accidents? The Fault Versus No-Fault Insurance Debate*, Washington, D.C.: Georgetown University Press, 2002.

*Pinnick v. Cleary*, 360 Mass. 1, 271 N.E.2d 592, June 29, 1971.

Priest, George, "Why 'Auto Choice' Is a Lemon," *Wall Street Journal*, July 12, 1998, p. 14.

Public Law 93-637, Federal Trade Commission Improvement Act, January 4, 1975.

Public Law 99-272, Consolidated Omnibus Budget Reconciliation Act, April 7, 1986.

Rabin, Robert L., "The Historical Development of the Fault Principle: A Reinterpretation," *Georgia Law Review*, Vol. 15, 1981, pp. 925–962.

Rahdert, Mark C., *Covering Accident Costs: Insurance, Liability, and Tort Reform*, Philadelphia, Pa.: Temple University Press, 1995.

RAND Corporation, "Auto Personal Injury Compensation," last modified August 4, 2009. As of November 24, 2009:
http://www.rand.org/icj/pubs/auto.html

Reich, Kenneth, "Push Starts for No-Frills, No-Fault Car Insurance," *Los Angeles Times*, May 24, 1989a, pp. 1–3.

———, "Nader Draws Criticism by Consumers for No-Fault View," *Los Angeles Times*, May 28, 1989b, pp. 1–3.

Rhode Island General Laws, Title 9, Courts and Civil Procedure, Procedure Generally, Chapter 9-1, Causes of Action, Section 9-1-33, Insurer's Bad Faith Refusal to Pay a Claim Made Under Any Insurance Policy. As of December 1, 2009:
http://www.rilin.state.ri.us/Statutes/TITLE9/9-1/9-1-33.HTM

Rokes, Willis Park, *No-Fault Insurance*, Santa Monica, Calif.: Insurors Press, 1971.

Rollins, Weld A., "A Proposal to Extend the Compensation Principle to Accidents in the Streets," *Massachusetts Law Quarterly*, No. 4, 1919, pp. 392 et seq.

Rolph, John E., James K. Hammitt, Robert L. Houchens, and Sandra Segal Polin, *Automobile Accident Compensation*, Vol. I: *Who Pays How Much How Soon?* Santa Monica, Calif.: RAND Corporation, R-3050-ICJ, 1985. As of October 29, 2009:
http://www.rand.org/pubs/reports/R3050/

Rosenfield, Harvey, "Auto Insurance: Crisis and Reform," *University of Memphis Law Review*, Vol. 29, Fall 1998, pp. 69–135.

Ross, H. Laurence, *Settled Out of Court: The Social Process of Insurance Claims Adjustment*, 2nd ed., New York: Aldine Publishing Company, 1980.

Royse, David, "Florida Legislature Passes No-Fault Car Insurance for Jan. 1 Return," *Insurance Journal*, October 6, 2007. As of December 7, 2009:
http://www.insurancejournal.com/news/southeast/2007/10/06/84095.htm

Ryan, Lewis C., and Bruno H. Green, "Pedestrianism: A Strange Philosophy," *ABA Journal*, Vol. 42, 1956, pp. 117–183.

S. 837—*see* U.S. Senate (1999).

Saskatchewan Statutes, Chapter 38, Section 32.

———, Chapter 38, Section 69.

Schuck, Peter H., "Tort Reform Kiwi-Style," *Yale Law and Policy Review*, Vol. 27, No. 1, Fall 2008, pp. 187–204.

Schwartz, Gary T., "Tort Law and the Economy in Nineteenth-Century America: A Reinterpretation," *Yale Law Journal*, Vol. 90, No. 8, July 1981, pp. 1717–1775.

———, "The Character of Early American Tort Law," *UCLA Law Review*, Vol. 36, 1989, pp. 641–718.

———, "Auto No-Fault and First-Party Insurance: Advantages and Problems," *Southern California Law Review*, Vol. 73, No. 3, 2000, pp. 611–676.

Shavell, Steven, *Economic Analysis of Accident Law*, Cambridge, Mass.: Harvard University Press, 1987.

Sherman, P. Tecumseh, *A Criticism of Proposals for Compulsory Motor Vehicle Compensation Insurance*, New York: National Association of Casualty and Surety Executives, 1929.

———, "Grounds for Opposing the Automobile Accident Compensation Plan," *Law and Contemporary Problems*, Vol. 3, No. 4, October 1936, pp. 598–608.

Shinkman, Ronald, "No-Fault Auto Insurance Rises Again," *Los Angeles Business Journal*, April 10, 1995.

Shugerman, Jed Handelsman, "A Watershed Moment: Reversals of Tort Theory in the Nineteenth Century," *Journal of Tort Law*, Vol. 2, No. 1, January 2008, art. 2. As of December 1, 2009:
http://www.bepress.com/jtl/vol2/iss1/art2

Sloan, Frank A., Bridget A. Reilly, and Christoph M. Schenzler, "Tort Liability Versus Other Approaches for Deterring Careless Driving," *International Review of Law and Economics*, Vol. 14, No. 1, March 1994, pp. 53–71.

———, "Effects of Tort Liability and Insurance on Heavy Drinking and Drinking and Driving," *Journal of Law and Economics*, Vol. 38, No. 1, April 1995, pp. 49–78.

Smith, Eric, and Randall Wright, "Why Is Automobile Insurance in Philadelphia So Damn Expensive?" *American Economic Review*, Vol. 82, No. 4, September 1992, pp. 756–772.

Smith, Jeremiah, "Sequel to Workmen's Compensation Acts," *Harvard Law Review*, Vol. 27, No. 3, January 1914, pp. 235–259.

Smith, Young Berryman, Austin J. Lilly, and Noel Thomas Dowling, "Compensation for Automobile Accidents: A Symposium," *Columbia Law Review*, Vol. 32, No. 5, 1932, pp. 785–824.

Stewart, Richard, "Automobile Insurance Reform," testimony before the Joint Legislative Committee on Insurance Rates, Regulation and Recodification of the Insurance Law, New York, April 29, 1970. As of November 25, 2009: http://www.stewarteconomics.com/SEI-docs/Publications/Automobile%20 Insurance%20Reform.pdf

Stewart, Richard E., and Barbara D. Stewart, "The Loss of the Certainty Effect," *Risk Management and Insurance Review*, Vol. 4, No. 2, 2001, pp. 29–49. As of December 1, 2009: http://www.stewarteconomics.com/Certainty%20Effect.pdf

Studdert, David M., and Troyen A. Brennan, "No-Fault Compensation for Medical Injuries: The Prospect for Error Prevention," *Journal of the American Medical Association*, Vol. 286, No. 1, July 11, 2001, pp. 217–223.

Sugarman, Stephen D., "Quebec's Comprehensive Auto No-Fault Scheme and the Failure of Any of the United States to Follow," *Les Cahiers de Droit*, Vol. 39, June–September 1998.

*Sukup v. State*, 19 N.Y.2d 519, 227 N.E.2d 842, Ct. App. N.Y., May 16, 1967.

Svenson, Ola, "Are We All Less Risky and More Skillful Than Our Fellow Drivers?" *Acta Psychologica*, Vol. 47, No. 2, February 1981, pp. 143–148.

Talty, Stephan, *Empire of Blue Water: Captain Morgan's Great Pirate Army, the Epic Battle for the Americas, and the Catastrophe That Ended the Outlaws' Bloody Reign*, Waterville, Maine.: Thorndike Press, 2007.

Tennessee Code, Title 56, Insurance, Chapter 7, Policies and Policyholders, Part 1, General Provisions, Section 56-7-105, Additional Liability upon Insurers and Bonding Companies for Bad-Faith Failure to Pay Promptly.

Tijms, Henk, *Understanding Probability: Chance Rules in Everyday Life*, Cambridge, Mass.: Cambridge University Press, 2007.

U.S. Department of Labor, Bureau of Labor Statistics, *1995 Consumer Expenditure Survey*, Washington D.C.: Government Printing Office, 1997.

U.S. Department of Transportation, *Driver Behavior and Accident Involvement: Implications for Tort Liability*, Washington D.C., 1970.

———, *Compensating Auto Accident Victims: A Follow-Up Report on No-Fault Auto Insurance Experiences*, Washington, D.C.: Office of the Secretary of Transportation, DOT-P-30-84-20, May 1985.

———, *Highway Statistics Summary to 1995*, Washington, D.C.: Public Roads Administration, Federal Highway Administration, 2003. As of October 30, 2009: http://www.fhwa.dot.gov/ohim/summary95/

U.S. House of Representatives, Auto Choice Reform Act of 1999, referred to U.S. House of Representatives Subcommittee on Finance and Hazardous Materials, May 6, 1999. As of November 25, 2009:
http://www.thomas.gov/cgi-bin/bdquery/z?d106:HR01475:

U.S. Senate, Auto Choice Reform Act of 1999, S.837, hearing held, U.S. Senate Committee on Commerce, June 9, 1999. As of November 25, 2009:
http://www.thomas.gov/cgi-bin/bdquery/z?d106:SN00837:

Viaene, Stijn, Guido Dedene, and Richard A. Derrig, "Auto Claim Fraud Detection Using Bayesian Learning Neural Networks," *Expert Systems with Applications*, Vol. 29, No. 3, October 2005, pp. 653–666.

Victoria Statutes, Titles 60 and 61, Chapter 37, 1897.

*Washington v. Baxter*, 553 Pa. 434, 719 A.2d 733, October 29, 1998.

Widiss, Alan I., *Uninsured and Underinsured Motorist Insurance*, 2nd ed., Cincinnati, Ohio: Anderson Publishing Company, 1985.

Widiss, Alan I., J. Little, R. Clark, and T. Jones, *No-Fault Automobile Insurance in Action: The Experiences in Massachusetts, Florida, Delaware, and Michigan*, Dobbs Ferry, N.Y.: Oceana Publications, 1977.

Wisconsin Administrative Code, Chapter 6, Insurance, Section 6.11, Insurance Claim Settlement Practices.

Wisconsin Statutes, Chapter 344, Vehicles: Financial Responsibility, Subchapter II, Security for Past Accidents, Section 344.14, Suspension for Failure to Deposit Security; Impoundment of Vehicle; Exceptions. As of November 24, 2009:
http://nxt.legis.state.wi.us/nxt/gateway.dll?f=templates&fn=default.htm&d=stats&jd=344.14

———, Chapter 632, Insurance Contracts in Specific Lines, Subchapter III, Liability Insurance in General, Section 632.22, Required Provisions of Liability Insurance Policies.

Zador, Paul, and Adrian Lund, "Re-Analyses of the Effects of No-Fault Auto Insurance on Fatal Crashes," *Journal of Risk and Insurance*, Vol. 53, No. 2, June 1986, pp. 226–241.

Zoffer, H. Jerome, *The History of Automobile Liability Insurance Rating*, Pittsburgh, Pa.: University of Pittsburgh Press, 1959.

Zucco, Tom, "Repeal No-Fault Law, Say Insurers," *St. Petersburg (Fla.) Times*, March 4, 2006. As of December 7, 2009:
http://www.sptimes.com/2006/03/04/Business/Repeal_no_fault_law__.shtml

Zycher, Benjamin, "Automobile Insurance Regulation, Direct Democracy, and the Interests of Consumers," *CATO Review of Business and Government*, Vol. 13, No. 2, 1990, pp. 67–77. As of November 25, 2009:
http://www.cato.org/pubs/regulation/regv13n2/v13n2-8.pdf

Made in the USA
Coppell, TX
17 October 2024